# The Best Place in the World to Retire? Boquete, Panamá!

LIve for Less in Paradise!

Guru on the Volcano Series

Book 1

Dr. Timothy Zellmer

Dr. Timothy Zellmer

General Delivery

Boquete, Chiriquí

Republic of Panama, 0413

Website: www.timothyzellmer.com

Email: tim@imdrz.com

# Contents

1.
2.
3.
4.
5.
6.
7.
8.
9.
10.
11.
12.
13.
14.
15.
16.
17.
18.
19.
20.
21.
22.
23.
24.
25.
26.
27.
28.
29.
30.

# Bonus eBook

To help guide you through retirement in Boquete, Panama, I created a free bonus companion course that includes a consultation and referral with a $250 per person or $500 per couple credit to Migration Attorneys, discounted hotel stay, and travel guidance. Plus you get a great new video interview with my Attorney explaining the recent changes to legal residency. Getting the Free eBook is your first step toward success with the content in this book, so I highly recommend you get it now. The supplemental materials in this free ebook are 4-steps that can be completed in as little as 4-weeks, making it easy to take action as you read along.

See you in Boquete!

Get Free Ebook:

*"How To Retire In Paradise In As Little As 4-Weeks—No Spanish Needed—Even If You've Never Left The Country."*

Visit the following link to download your Free eBook now:

https://www.timothyzellmer.com/free-ebook.

# The Author

Hey there. I'm Dr. Timothy Zellmer but feel free to call me *Uncle Timmy* or *Tío Tim* around these parts. Growing up exposed to my grandpa's Hereford bull breeding ranch in the Dakotas, I was immersed in the vibrant cowboy-Indian culture next to two Indian Reservations, the Lower Brule and Crow Creek.

My path has led me from working as a cowboy dentist on those two Indian Reservations and many others to living with the *Ngäbe* tribe in Panama. I've evolved into a flexible entrepreneur and a committed humanitarian. I did it living in Boquete, Panama, where I've called home for 12 years.

I am the former President of the Rotary Club of Boquete. I loved working on community projects. One example is my "3 Little Rooms" initiative, which built an Indigenous High School on the beautiful Caribbean Island of Bastimientos.

Along with my community work, I've also entered hospitality. I built Hotel Central Boquete/Café Central, juggling roles from builder to barista.

You may know me as some kind of *Boquete Whisperer*. For years, I have posted videos of life in Boquete. Now, I'm diving into book publishing and taking on the title of *Author*.

Beyond my town, I'm dedicated to my life-saving nutrition research. I do it as a member of the Rotary EClub One. It's all about focusing on sustainable development and health.

My journey revolves around service, entrepreneurship, and creativity—a tale in progress. My joy filled life now comes from cherishing moments in Boquete while striving to make a positive impact in our ever-evolving world.

# Why I Wrote This Book

I penned this book in gratitude for my amazing life here, in Boquete, Panama. This is the best place in the world. The diverse mix of fascinating folks has me hooked. Nope, not the weather. It's the people.

It is a big vision—a series of books, Life Hacker Handbooks. I have been possessed by these ideas and driven to express them. I am here to serve the dream. From this first book's title, you can see that *Retirees* are the focus of the first book's message. But I'm also thinking of your *Grandkids*.

My best friend Kent and I leftafter graduating high school in 1977. The next week, we were newly minted pioneers of long-distance backpacking on the Appalachian Trail. We soon discovered the need for hitchhiking and the strange energy of backpacker hostels. These books manifest that same peculiar force.

We liked the hyper-helpful hiker-hoteliers. I would often daydream of having a Hostel on the AT. Back then, on the trail, we called it the *Miracle of the Day*. Now it's called *Trail Magic*. Everyone sees you doing your hard-thing. They are so attracted to that. People help or join up when you are living life aligned with a vision. Writing is my hard-thing now.

Hitch to town, find the Hostel, clean up, do laundry, get food, shuttle or hitch back to the trail, put on a backpack and walk, treat water, camp, eat, sleep, and start over. What life paths would those two backpackers have taken with a copy of the Guru on the Volcano Series onboard?

It's the *Hero's Journey*. It is the call and the refusal of the call. It keeps knocking on my door over and over again throughout my life. My challenge now is to tell my best stories. Point the way forward. Keep going. One book after another. "You can do it!"

# Introduction

## Panamá Loco

You can read all the books about being here. Like *Jimmy Buffett's* song, "*First Look*," exploring your options should be exciting. Your first look might be all it takes to go *Panamá Loco!* He sings the truth in that song. A person prepares for an adventure with language tapes and books, but nothing can prepare them for what they experience on arrival.

*Warning!* If you read this book, you may develop severe wanderlust or a weird craving for adventure. Some strange thoughts may enter your mind. This *Panamá Loco* thing, this condition, is contagious. Be warned now. You can experience contact with the contagion online. I need your informed consent to proceed.

Use X, Y, and Z search terms to receive an offer of a blue and red pill. You can take only one. *Red pill* - you risk learning a challenging, unsettling truth. And your life freaks out forever. Some people see this stuff and flip. Take the *Blue pill* –stay contented with the experience of ordinary reality. - the analogy of *The Matrix*

You may get lit and launched like a rocket up off that *Lazy-Boy* chair you are surfing and go surfing for real. Or you could go boogie boarding, you know, in short waves. It is safer that way, like where I love to go, down at *Las Lajas Beach.* That is here in *Chiriqui* province. Boquete is in this province. That lovely beach spot is an hour and 40 minutes away. The *Las Lajas Beach Resort* has boogie boards for rent and day passes. Damn! Now you have no excuses for not livin-da-dream!

You may find yourself at a life-size crossroads as you gaze upon the horizon ahead. You have some hard choices to make. Having spent a lifetime toiling away, sweet retirement beckons. You are finally free to decide your schedule. Taste it! Acquaint yourself again with freedom! You can manage your day as you see fit. Time is yours.

You want to make the most of it. You start ordering your affairs and creating a plan. You begin to think that life is starting to look up.

Retirement? Big dreams are calling. Friends and family want to see you. Daydream destinations call out. Hope sustains you—visions of a beautiful retirement inch closer to reality.

That vision is different for everyone. For some retirees, it means - a time to reflect, grow, and even finally flourish in new and exciting ways. For others, it ignites a burning desire to forge ahead into the next adventure of their lives.

Regardless of your chosen path, cherish and refine it. Pursue it. It's time to be serious about your dreams! Be careful spending your freedom coins.

You now realize *it's later than you think* andhave a few new concerns. Yes, retirement presents unique challenges. The way you lived before retiring may no longer be practical. Significant changes are rushing towards you. Your worries cast long shadows over your plans.

Is it the money? Your income may be going down at a time when expenses are going up. The price of housing, cars, health, and medications stresses you out. The *little accountant in your head* worries about the budget and size of your precious dreams.

But the reason you are reading this book may be about something other than money. Could it be *breathlessness*? Are you one of the many suffering from forest fires far away? So many cities had record-setting air pollution events this last year. I know that was hard on people. Sometimes, the smoke stayed too long.

My sister sent me a curious photo of what I thought was a streetlight in the night. She said, "No, Timmy! That was smoke from Canada's forest fires. It smells like burning plastic! I took that picture in front of our house at noon yesterday." Wow! Skies, blacker than night, over Sioux City, Iowa!

Do heat waves, hurricanes, droughts, or floods affect your health? Distressing stories are on all the news channels. Are conditions getting worse where you live? No, you're not imagining it. Consider this news for a moment. It hit 37.8°C (100°F) in the middle of South America's winter! Unfortunately, the Amazon is currently going through the worst drought ever recorded. And you know what? There's a genuine concern that this critical region might be on the edge of a tipping point.

Consider this odd new question. Can you get insurance for a new home if you move? Hey folks, I have some breaking news for you! In California, it's getting hard to get a new home insured. There are signs of a similar trend happening in Florida. It is like that song. "Oh, the times - they are - changing."

Migrant waves are flowing like never before. You know what's interesting? There's a big trend happening around the world. More people are moving from cities to the suburbs or even to different countries. It's like a whole new way of life! Are we ready to see tens of thousands of U.S. citizens working via the Internet but living in Mexico City? Whole neighborhoods now look like little America!

Almost half of office workers started working from home during the pandemic. Now, companies are struggling to get them to return to the office. Those with international roots were the first to consider leaving. Now it is everyone! We all had plenty of time on our hands. The volume of searches for *International Living* skyrocketed. That's when many of you discovered the search term *Boquete*. Did you go down that rabbit hole?

## Live for Less in Paradise, Retired

The irresistible charms are perfect temperatures, flawless weather, and pristine air quality. Boquete has a slang term here: *Bajareque*. That means the sun shines on you while hitting you with mist. That means rainbow weather country, or what you might call paradise.

We have affordable housing, reasonable healthcare, and reliable public transportation. Nearby beaches are great for spontaneous day trips. Leave the highland's spring-like climate with green cloud forests and go to the beach for the day. You could also go to an island.

You might have stumbled upon pictures of our flourishing coffee plantations. They look like blooming flowers at every corner, a dream come true. Do it sooner. Take early retirement to get Panama's amazing discounts!

Wow, you've made it this far! Thank you for your time and attention. You enjoy thinking outside the box and aren't afraid to question things. You and I have that in common!

Chapter 1
# Perpetual Spring

## No Need for A/C or Furnace in Boquete

Boquete hides in the embrace of the *Talamanca Mountains*. It enjoys eden-like weather. This mountain range forms the continental divide and passes north of our town. The weather report here is like "Goldilocks" trying porridge. Here, we like it not too hot and not too cold. We want it *just right.*

I balanced that with the knowledge that I had lived for years in some remote, rugged country in Montana. I was into extreme snowmobiling. In winter, my horse wore spiked shoes for ice. I loved the lifestyle and all the wild weather that goes with ranch life up in the mountains. When it pours down here, I often say, "Looks like the best day of the year back in Montana!" And I mean it.

It is hard to believe, but most homes do not have central heating or cooling. Boquete has an average afternoon temperature reading of 22.2°C (72°F) and little deviation from this. You can keep your windows open for most of the day. But when the chill sets in at dusk, it's time to close them up.

## Better Gear and Clothes

The rain usually comes straight down. I wear waterproof boots or river sandals during rainy days and have an extra-sized umbrella nearby. Raincoats and pants are excellent additions when it blows hard or rains sideways. Or wait it out and have a hot chocolate!

My Viking ancestors had a saying: "*There is no such thing as bad weather, just bad clothes.*" I love minimalism, ultralight travel, and high-quality equipment. You need jungle stuff, tried-and-true gear, and clothing. Get ready for your new life in Boquete.

Most days, all I need is my favorite ¾ zip fleece sweater. When I launch before dawn in the mornings, it goes on zipped up. It comes off once the chill goes away, then it's back on in the evening. I tie it around my neck or waist when it warms or toss it into my small 4x4. Whether I head off to a remote location or stay in town doesn't matter.

**ProTip:** Layer up or be ready to. Conditions here in Boquete can vary from moment to moment. Steer clear of cotton shirts and blue jeans! They get drenched and drag you down, leaving you freezing. *Quick-dry* clothing is the way to go. It keeps you warm when wet. Boquete receives 115 to 200 inches of rain per year.

You can bet my trusty red *Mystery Ranch - Urban Assault 19-liter backpack* will be by my side. It's perfect to keep my laptop inside. I can be random. You can find me working on my writing or editing videos in odd places.

I recommend Mystery Ranch backpacks and gear. I'm a super fan of *Dana Gleason*, one of the two founders. He's the reason I moved to Montana. I met him in the late 90s at *Appalachian Trail Days* in Damascus, Virginia. That pack is *my everyday carry*.

In my little 4x4 Suzuki Jimny, I keep an extra layer for upper body protection. I have a *Polar Guard* vest with a simple water-resistant surface. I keep it as a rain cover for my base layer of 3/4 fleece. Polar Guard is good stuff, made for the U.S. military. It is lightweight. It breathes. If you fall in the river, take it off and ring it out. That will restore most of the insulating qualities.

# Ventilation, Fans, and Dehumidifiers

Most homes have ceiling fans or pedestal fans. People leave their windows open all day. But if you get home in the dark of the night, it may be a bit chilly inside. Some Panamanian-style homes use vented cinder blocks for the top of the walls. These blocks have screens to keep out bugs and allow the air to circulate. It's a way to keep the house fresh and bug-free without condensation on the windows and walls.

*Drips and wetness from condensation + Mold Spores = Furry Walls.* Closed-up homes can become overwhelmed if not maintained. Open Architecture and vented storage are the norm here. The humid air sneaks in, and the night chills the windows and walls, causing condensation. I used to wake up with wet walls. Ventilation or running dehumidifiers are essential here in a closed-up place.

You may occasionally encounter homes with cute little ceramic space heaters, electric blankets, and heating pads. Locals know how to keep cozy in style! Life is too short to catch yourself a chill, so it's nice to have something to take the nip off.

**ProTip:** Dehumidifiers also give off a little heat. I've had one for two years and use it daily. It's rugged and large, while the tiny ones need frequent dumping. It is a *Frigidaire* product. The warmth it gives off feels great. Bid farewell to that evening chill. It also safeguards your home from mold, mildew, and allergies caused by their growth. It's a game-changer!

## Dry and Wet Seasons

Let's clear up some confusing terms locals use for the seasons here. First, when it's *summer* up north, guess what? It's called *winter* here. The second thing to learn is that in Panama, we call the warmer, dry season *summer*. Here's the third thing: they call the wet season *winter in Panama*. I know it can get confusing.

The country's dry season (called summer in Panama) runs from mid-December to mid-April. If you plan to visit during these five months, you'll be happy to know that most of Panama is sunny and dry. Yet, the Caribbean coast may see some rain. If it's raining in Boquete, it will likely be sunny in Bocas del Toro, and vice versa.

**ProTip**: The driest periods in Bocas del Toro Province are September-October and February-March.

Do you know what's interesting about Panama? Some areas are contrarians. The western highlands, Bocas del Toro, and much of the Caribbean coast are good examples. They don't follow the typical dry and rainy seasons. Panama has a unique climatic pattern.

Some areas have microclimates that receive rainfall at any time of the year. Recently, the weather seasons have been unpredictable. They have deviated from their usual patterns all year. It's a good idea to be ready for these ups and downs.

Boquete is in the western highlands next to Costa Rica. It is about 14 miles (22.3 Km) away by a straight line from a corner of Costa Rica that extends from the crooked border. Boquete is at the top of the map of Chiriqui Province. It is all the way north in the direction of the Caribbean. Boquete's rivers drain south into the Pacific Ocean.

Above us lies the majestic Continental Divide. It serves as the boundary of the neighboring province of Bocas del Toro. Their rivers run into the warm waters of the Caribbean Sea. That sea is part of the Atlantic Ocean waters. Bocas is the Panamanian area with thousands of idyllic Caribbean islands.

*ProTip*: Discover the local geography. Look up a map of *The Republic of Panama*. Notice it looks like a big "S " sitting on a short stool that fell backward. See that Costa Rica is on the left (West), and The Caribbean Seas of the Atlantic Ocean is at the top (North). Columbia is on the right side of the map (East). And the Pacific Ocean is at the bottom (South). It is a quarter turn counterclockwise of what you would expect.

# Chiriqui Province

This Panamanian Province (*Chiriqui*) has many microclimates, making generalization challenging. The valley of Boquete alone has over 150 microclimates. The Highlands of Panama are tiny compared to our neighbors, Costa Rica and Columbia. Those two countries have prominent highland sanctuaries. So, ours are unique to Panamanian people.

From mid-April to mid-December, the rainy season takes hold. During this season, we usually get massive bursts of rain in the afternoon or early evening. It can be a real downer if you fail to prepare.

**ProTip:** The folks here are big fans of early mornings. They make the most of the sunny start to the day, dodging the afternoon rain. Some even wake up before dawn to enjoy a walk or get work done outside. They know the seasonal downpours usually hit around 2 pm or 4 pm. Check your watch when it starts raining in the afternoon. You will see how often it is spot on.

## Local Customs

Come and enjoy a delightful Spanish tradition. After a late lunch, take a moment to yourself as the afternoon rain rolls in. It's a perfect way to relax and recharge! Embrace the local way of life with a short afternoon nap, known as a *Siesta, after your midday meal*. Give yourself two hours to recharge and let the rain pass. Then, head out on a sunset stroll or a night adventure.

Seek refuge from the afternoon heat and humidity. Create a shaded porch adorned with a spacious, matrimonial-size hammock. Or pick an iced coffee drink in my coffee shop and head to my hotel's backyard oasis. The balcony and back terrace are so peaceful, filled with cozy hammocks. They are waiting for you to relax and enjoy. Try it out during an afternoon shower on our covered balcony. It will put you right to sleep.

You can find those hammocks at the David Fair in February. They're the perfect size for two adults and a little kiddo to chill in. Not only are they well-made, but they're also super affordable. It's wild how they bring them here as part of an international caravan. You must keep them dry to avoid mold; our sun will also damage them. They come from Nicaragua. They are famous for low-cost, large-timbered, hardwood furniture. It is heavy-duty.

Panama's temperature varies depending on the location. In the lowlands, temperatures range between 32°C (90°F) during the day and 21 21°C (70°F) at night. The highlands offer cooler weather, with an average daily temperature of around 20°C (68°F). It can drop to as low as 10°C (50°F) at higher elevations.

At the summit of our Volcan Baru, it can drop below freezing 0°C (32°F). It's notorious for testing the endurance of those brave souls who make the ascent. They usually do it in the dark to witness the sunrise at the top. That's because 15 or 20 minutes after sunrise, the clouds commonly drop and block the view. It has been quite treacherous at times, catching climbers off guard. Freezing rain and gusty winds can appear out of thin air! So prepare yourself for possible arctic conditions.

I have a friend from Canada. I nicknamed him *The Mountain Man*. He comes yearly for the dry season- a real snowbird, you know? Last year, he rented a cozy little cabin right at the entrance of Volcan Baru National Park. I spent two days and nights with him. We did some excellent bird-watching and off-trail hikes. The views were incredible. You can look down over town from high above. I had to wear three layers. I wore a long-sleeved shirt, a 3/4 fleece pullover, and a stocking cap. Then, when the sun went behind the volcano, I added a down jacket!

## Sunshine and Clean Air

Boquete enjoys abundant sunshine all year round. February is the sunniest month, with almost eight hours of sun daily. Gentle clouds often go with the sunshine.

Here's a fun fact for you! Do you know what's interesting about the equator and Panama? The equator is very close. It is only 1000 Km (600 miles) to the south. So there is a slight difference between the longest and shortest days of the year. It's only one hour and three minutes long! The summer and winter Solstices mark the longest and shortest days of the year. Through the seasons, days don't vary much in length. That is because the equator is so very close.

Crazy, right? The last place I lived in the U.S. was Great Falls, Montana. During the Winter Solstice, there are only 8 hours and 26 minutes of daylight. On the Summer Solstice, there are a whopping

15 hours and 58 minutes! That's a tremendous 7-hour difference between the longest and shortest days. The longest and shortest days differ a lot. The significant difference in day length throughout the year happens because the equator is far away.

So, Boquete experiences little change in day length throughout the year. The consistent day length lasts all year. It makes Boquete, and all of Panama, the perfect cure for S.A.D. (Seasonal Affective Disorder). S.A.D. is a dangerous wintertime depression affecting those closer to the Earth's poles.

In Panama, the annual variation in sunrise and sunset is half an hour. You will see that the sun and moon rise and set more straight up and down than at an angle. You need a flashlight at sundown if you're in the woods. The complete darkness of night can come on fast! That's how people get lost. Dawn happens the same. Take comfort in knowing that you can always witness a full moon rise! It occurs within a few minutes.

Boquete has fantastic air quality, free of air pollution. Its unbeatable freshness makes you feel alive, you know? Every breath you take with floral fragrances. It also has the irresistible aroma of freshly roasted coffee. Being surrounded by the "lungs of the world" is a plus. Our cloud forests and rainforests work 24/7 to purify our air here in Panama.

But let's be honest. Boquete could be better. A few grass and forest fires can happen, and dust, mold, and mildew may cause discomfort if you have allergies. Depending on your location, the windy, dry season days can kick up dust. Like many, I have a HEPA-grade air filter in my bedroom at night, particularly during the wet season. I also have a link for the one I like on my website.

**ProTip:** Did your allergies blow up on arrival? Talk to a qualified Medical Doctor first. But every day, I take the antihistamine called *Zyrtec* or the generic daily. It is lower in price here. This medication and the generic analogs are 24-hour antihistamines. It is safer for people with a heart condition, like me. It is available without a prescription. For some unknown reason, it has been much less expensive than the generics sold here lately. Also, *Phena-Taps* is an ephedra-like decongestant and antihistamine medication. It costs about one dollar for three tablets. It is available without a prescription. Check with your doctor first.

During the windy season, some areas can get pretty dusty. We know that February, in particular, is our windiest month. Let me share a funny story with you. A few years back, I had the opportunity to assist a recently widowed, elderly German lady. She decided to sell her farm in Costa Rica and move across the border. I often help my friends find great renters for their properties in this area. And guess what? I connected her with a buddy from the Rotary Club who had rentals.

The next time I bumped into her, she told me, "You won't believe it! I've made friends with the boys who live downhill. They've been so kind to retrieve my lawn chairs daily. The strong gusts of wind keep sending them tumbling down the hill. They end up stuck in the boys' fence!"

But, everything is calm from the start of May through mid-December. I love the pungent spring-has-sprung smell from the first rain after a dry spell - it's divine! Nothing is quite like it. And we get some great lightning storms. They can add the fragrance of sharp ozone. This year, my friends and I couldn't stop raving about the heavenly scent in the air

Chapter 2
# Live for Less

## Cheap Food

Come to any of our three local *Sabroson Restaurants* for a morning treat. Try a half-order of liver and onions with peppers. Add the local *Fry Bread* or *Hojaldre (Puff Pastry)*, which sounds like *o-haul-drah,* for less than $2.50. Not a fan of liver? They also offer delicious eggs or chopped steak in gravy or wieners in red sauce for about the same price. You can ask for meat sauce on top of your Hojaldre. They won't charge extra.

Indulge in a cost-effective lifestyle at Boquete, Panama. You must delve into the local cuisine to bask in the authentic Panamanian experience. A must-try on your culinary adventure is the national soup called *Sancocho*. It is very cheap. This delectable and hearty soup goes well with a small plate of white rice. You find it at every corner for less than two dollars. Trust me, this dish will please your palate. It will fill you up and rehydrate you. To spice things up, add a touch of the local hot sauce.

**Pro-Tip**: Look (or ask them!) where the taxi drivers eat. They know local prices and food quality.

I want to inform you about *Canasta Básica,* or *the basic food basket.* The government decrees to keep basic food prices low. They do this to reduce the misery of poor Panamanians. Look for the little sign next to these items: Lentils, beans, rice, eggs, chicken, hamburger, milk, and pork. The displayed sign shows they take part in the program. But, the little signs may be missing. Ask at the grocery stores if you need clarification about *Control de Precio*. These are under *Price Control.* They will be happy to show you.

An article on www.newsroompanama.com states that a little over four million citizens live in Panama. (4,337,768 reported in 2022. Half are in Panama City.) Of these, 287,000 live in extreme poverty and cannot afford the basic food basket. Extreme poverty is having an income of less than $330 per month for an average family of five. "They barely have enough money to buy some food." People in poverty here earn over $330 but less than $630.50 monthly.

The Ministry of Economy and Finance (MEF) calculates two basic food basket prices. In June 2023, they calculated the cost at $345.83. In September 2023, they reported the second. The Authority for Consumer Protection and Defense of the Competition (ACODECO) calculates it. They have three ranges: the most expensive ($326.75), the average ($291.18), and the least costly ($271.16).

Food basket calculations don't include other costs. These include regular household and personal expenses but don't include cleaning supplies, water, health, education, housing, or electricity. I don't want to bum you out, but I want to expose you to interesting things you may never notice here.

I wish to give you a glimpse into two phenomena in Panama. First, you can see why food is affordable whether you cook at home or eat out. Also, foreign-born retirees often feel a solid connection to underprivileged kids. Many go above and beyond to support child education.

I've seen many heartwarming and tear-jerking situations. Generous ex-pats ensure that Panamanian children get the education they deserve. While the country offers scholarships to most needy kids, it doesn't cover all the costs. For example, many kids don't attend school because they lack the required school uniform.

If you're out for a splurge, venture to *Restaurant Row* for one of Boquete's world-class restaurants. You can find sumptuous cuisine for under $30 per person, including drinks. If you stay at my hotel, you're a hop, skip, and jump away. You can't miss it. *My neighborhood favorites are Butcher Chop House, Retrogusto, Tacos Rudos, and La Posada La Boqueteña*. Do you want to talk? Take me out to one of those fine establishments!

My Hotel/Coffee Shop is a good night or day hang out with food service. We are famous for our $3.95 BLT Sandwich (bacon, lettuce, and tomato). It's cheap and delicious. We make it with fancy seed bread fried in butter. You can have it with or without an egg. We are the last stop on Restaurant Row, heading north at the start of the *Los Naranjos (The Orange Trees)* area.

Look for the giant-butterfly-shaped flower display. It has green grass sod and irrigation—installation on the left. You have passed the restaurant row and my hotel if you see it.

This dining district is bursting with exquisite food. It also offers live music at three locations now. Additionally, warm fireplaces are in the bar at the back of the *Panamonte Hotel*. They will keep you cozy during your meal. The row is the hottest spot in the country. You can immerse yourself in this world-class destination without paying the prices of Paris or Hong Kong!

There's nothing better in the mornings than the enticing smell of baked bread. Bakeries offer *Pan de Piso* - ten hot, incredible buns with hard, crunchy crusts for about a dollar! The name pan de piso is intriguing since "piso" in Spanish means floor. Is the crust as hard as the floor? Well, people call them that.

Nothing is better than the soft *Pan-Machita (Blond Bread)* rolls. The best is the *Huevo (Egg)* version. They cost the same. Eat them when they are warm! With each bite, they melt in your mouth. I love shaping them into little canoes and filling them with sausage, eggs, butter, and jam. You can still buy them with only a thin dime; they are divine.

Don't miss out on trying the small *Indian Fry Bread* called *Hojaldras*. They cost about thirty cents. The best are at *Malu Restaurant* and the *Sandwich Shop.* They puff them up like billowy *Sopapillas*, the famous sugar-coated treat from Mexico. I like to fill my Hojaldras with butter and honey for dessert.

Our valley produces terrific honey. Find the *Butterfly House* with the Bee and Honey tours. That is my friend Emily's place. It's located a 15-minute walk past my hotel, going north. Then, right before the road splits, she is on the right. Don't miss out on what she's doing. Volunteers help raise her rare butterflies. Notice the high-tech lab. The butterfly house contains many rare species, including the famous *Blue Morpho*. They are the most beautiful butterflies in the world. You might spot one anywhere in our valley.

Be sure to quench your thirst with the artisanal, must-try drink called *Chicha*. It is a beautiful and inexpensive treat made with crushed fruit, raspadura *(abrasion),* (a natural cane sugar cake) made with water. *Raspadura* (or *Hard to Grate*) is the brown hockey pucks of pure cane sugar. This refreshing drink is available in *Soursop*. In Spanish, that is *Guanábana.* It is a vanilla ice cream-tasting fruit that is a traditional treatment for heartburn, stomach aches, diarrhea, and parasites.

Guanábana fruit can be larger than your head! It is green, like an avocado, with sharp spikes. *Starfruit* goes by the names *Fruta China* or *Fruta de Estrella.* My personal favorites are *Zarzamora (Blackberry) and Frambuesa (Raspberry).* Choose a small one and pay only $1.00, or go for a large one for about $1.50. It is amazing. Don't confuse it with *Chicheme* because that is different. That is a thick corn-based drink sold hot and cold, even bottled for sale in grocery stores.

Guys and gals, you've got to try Panama's traditional *Fried Foods* or *Frituras*. They are very economical and delicious. You'll find everything from savory meatballs and smoked meats to crispy snacks. Here, they call fried ground corn disks *Tortillas.* Don't let that confuse you. They call the *fried snake-shaped ground yellow spring-corn* treats *Almojábanos.* They are wonderful.

The next town below us is *Dolega.* They have an annual *Almojábanos Festival!* Skinny on the ends, shaped like a squiggly snake, and thick and long as a man's index finger. They are wonderful! Stuffed *Empanadas* come with pork, beef, or cheese. Once you taste *Frituras*, you will become hooked!

**ProTip**: Don't wait! Eat your Frituras where you get them. They are at their best, hot and fresh out of the kitchen - it's pure bliss!

So, are you craving this delicious late-night snack? Look no further than *Danni's Kiosco (Kiosk)!* It is before the river bridge. It's past the right split in the road, after the turn for the butterfly house. Then it is on the left side. It is on the way to *Bambuda Castle* (about a half mile uphill or north of Hotel Central Boquete). Trust me, it's worth the pit stop. When you arrive, ask for the one-of-everything pack I named the *Tio Tim Especial* or the *Uncle Timmy Special*. You can thank me later. I should be getting frequent flier miles there.

## Public Transportation

Public transportation offers a cost-effective solution for getting around. For only $1.75, you can get between Boquete and David in one hour. Here are some insider tips to consider when taking a taxi.

If you're a regular in town, the *Colectivo (Collective)* or share-a-taxi system is the way to go. Ask the driver, "Colectivo?" If he says yes, then hop on board! Remember, though, an answer of "no" or "*Privado*" *(Private)* means it's a one-customer-at-a-time taxi. It costs more but gets you to your destination without stopping.

It can be tricky for newcomers. Once you're used to it, you can join the shared taxi action like everyone else! Many colectivo taxis have set times and routes they take. The locals go to work at fixed times daily. All taxis, Colectivo and Privado, look the same. They are yellow-colored taxis.

**ProTip:** Foreign visitors and retirees get upset when they think they overpay for taxi rides. Stay clear. Memorize the question, *"Colectivo?"* Then, make your informed choice to save on fares!

Let's clarify some more confusion. The David bus lands at the *Parque Central (Central Park)* fountain and town clock area. Many newcomers need clarification. That bus disembarks there but departs elsewhere.

I have told hundreds of confused people where to go. The David bus leaves from the opposite park corner near the *Oficina de Correos (Post Office)*. Grab the bus at your convenience. They vamoose every 30 to 45 minutes. They keep a schedule and don't wait until the bus is full.

Also, you can catch the little neighborhood/mountain and valley buses. They are the big vans at *La Bruña* grocery store, which is only one block north (toward my hotel) of Central Park. If you live in the *Jaramillo* area, those colectivo taxis gather in front of the Romero Grocery store. Get your fare ready before hopping on board—planning is the key! Or stick a handful of change out, and they will pick the correct amount. They won't cheat you.

## Internet, Cable, Electricity, and Propane

What do Internet and Cable cost? Bringing the Internet to your smartphone, apartment, or home is inexpensive in Panama. I have paid much, much more in other places I have lived.

I used to buy the $5 scratch cards. I entered the tiny numbers to refill my cell phone. I bought them at the grocery stores and often asked the bagmen to do it. But now I have auto-pay with *Tigo Movil*. It costs me $39.22/month. That provides me with a *Hot Spot*. It is WiFi from my phone. That is how I log on and use the laptop computer I am writing this on now.

> **Pro Tip:** With a VPN (Virtual Private Network) you can see ALL the Amazon Prime Videos (Check out the "Fringe" series, I love it!) with your Amazon Prime account! I use, top rated NordVPN tuned to the good old U.S. of A.! And as a bonus you will be safe using coffee shop Free WiFi!

*Tigo* has good coverage, and I enjoy writing in the mountains above Boquete. Their main office is easy to find. It is next door to one of my favorite restaurants, *The Sandwich Shop.* They both have excellent service and bilingual help. The big guy at *Tigo* can answer your questions and fix your telephone problems. He is wonderful.

*You can get more help with phone and computer accessories at the Chino or electronics store. They are next to my virtual office, The Buckle Tip Coffee Studio.* They will serve you there while teaching you about our high-end specialty coffee. I'm there almost every day, usually in the morning. I love the young people at both locations and adopted all of them as my nieces and nephews. Both businesses are at the David Bus arrival spot (next to the town square's fountains and clock).

Many expats pay a person at the gringo market who sells and programs *Roku* or *Amazon Fire Sticks*. They are small USB devices that plug into the back of the newer TVs. Then, people can get all their favorite shows and news from where they came from. Adding your favorite cable channels, in packages or not, can be inexpensive. How much hockey my Canadian friends can get with these devices is astonishing!

Panama is lucky to have cheaper electricity than much of the world. Electricity is not expensive. It is often typical for household or apartment bills to amount to less than $30 per month. That's because we only need a little electricity. Air conditioning and heating are optional.

The Panamanian government subsidizes and controls the price of small propane tanks used for BBQ grills. It's pretty cool! Refilling those tank refills costs $5.37, making it super affordable. You own the tanks but can trade them in for a full one. If you want to buy a new cylinder from *Tropigas* or *Panagas*, you will pay between $40 and $65. Here's a little tip: You can purchase a new Tropigas tank at a lower price in David.

In Boquete, you'll find plenty of local spots to swap your empty small propane tank. These tanks are for stoves and instant-on, tankless water heaters, which are popular choices among Panamanian households. Local families often endure cold showers.

## Suicide Showers

They may also rely on *Electric Suicide Showers*. These function like an electric arc welder inside your shower head. They are plastic cases that the water passes through to give you a hot shower. You regulate the heat by increasing or decreasing the water flow. There may also be heat range settings you can adjust on it. Don't change the settings while it is running! Turn it off first.

I had a shocking incident in my teenage years. I visited a college roommate and his family for Christmas in Tegucigalpa, Honduras. They are pretty short people, and so was the house shower. Their suicide shower setup was an antique electrified one with bare wire attached to ceramic insulators—the same ones used on my grandpa's electric fence. You can guess what happened.

It zapped me; I got knocked out for a moment and crashed through their plastic sliding shower door. I could have died of embarrassment. I came back to life with shampoo in my eyes, naked, cradled in my college roommate's terrified mother's arms. Lol!.

So, a friendly reminder is in order. Be cautious! These devices look like giant plastic shower heads with electrical connections. They usually last only two to three years. Please! Please! Please! Have a licensed electrician inspect or install them before using them. And have them double-check they are grounded. Stay safe!

The giant shoulder-high propane tanks do not have regulated or reduced prices. There are delivery services available for homeowners' convenience. Some families choose to have two larger tanks to ensure they never run out of gas. When one tank is empty, turn it off. Then, slip the valve on and open the new tank. Go slow! It's a simple way to keep the gas flowing! I am also seeing short, fat, larger refillable tanks at businesses. That type is new. The large tanker trucks fill them with their long hoses.

## $.50 to see a Public Health Doctor.

If you don't have insurance, you'll have to shell out 50 cents to see a Medical Doctor at Public Health. Our local Social Security Clinic has modern digital X-rays, Dentists, etc. Boquete's Public and Social Security clinics have Pharmacies with considerable drug discounts.

It is worth noting that not all medications are available there. You may have to go to a private pharmacy; we have many. Some have 25% discount days every week. Some things still have government-subsidized discounts that started during the COVID-19 pandemic.

You may need to visit *Chiriqui Hospital in David* for prescribed medications. It is private and has a greater variety of medications available. They also have a medical doctor who can access the *Yellow Prescription Pads.* That's the only way you can get intense opioid pain relief, such as *Oxycodone.* Even *Morphine* for hospice care is very limited. Many people get their prescriptions filled in their home country. Then, they mail them here.

*Vicodin* (Hydrocodone with Tylenol) is not available by prescription in the country. Pain management may be possible in their Emergency Room. You may need to be under the care of an Orthopedic Surgeon or Internist. Panama restricts powerful, dangerous medicines like Oxycodone.

Panama never had a big pain pill problem like the U.S. because of these policies. I wish we had been as wise as Panama. Here, they restrict this group of pain management drugs. Please note that we may have a few medications unavailable here. If essential, this has caused many to leave.

You can find *Boquete's Public Health Clinic* on the corner next to *Romero's Grocery Store.* They treat sore throats, earaches, and stomach trouble. I have taken untold numbers of tourists with bug bites and bad sunburns. They are happy to help sick and injured people. It is a good place for lab work and stitches.

Foreigners think they can treat themselves, especially for diarrhea. Parasites can be the problem. The medicines prescribed in their home countries don't affect these parasites. Many end up needing IV rehydration because of their hard-headedness. If you're sick, go to the doctor! Ambulances are available for rides to David's Regional Public Hospital. They are also available to the Women's and Children's Hospitals.

# Zero Cost Births

I did not know that *Births are 100% Free of Charge!* I discovered that at *Maternity Hospital José Domingo de Obaldia.* It is also known as *Hospital Materno Infantil Jose Domingo de Obaldia.* They are fantastic at dealing with emergencies. They have Chiriqui province's Pediatric Neonatal Intensive Care Unit there.

*Dr. Newton Osborn* is my friend from the Rotary Club. He lives here and is *Chief of Women's Health and Infectious Diseases*. I am sure he runs a tight ship as tight as he did in the States. We are lucky to have such a talented medical doctor who protects provincial health.

A year ago, a husband and wife invited me to their home birth one night. Mom was not progressing. The baby wasn't coming out. Talk about a crisis! I've been night-calving and lambing on ranches, but we were over our heads.

That baby was breech! I dialed the police chief and asked him to call the checkpoint. We needed to go through without stopping. We ran in convoy with emergency flashers. I called *Dr. Chang* for an in-flight medical consultation. I also asked for directions to the right hospital and the new emergency entrance.

Great team effort, everyone! Thanks! You saved those two! As we rushed her in, in the middle of the night, I noticed a sign that read "*100% cost-free births*." Panama! What a country! I'm all raring to go at four in the morning!!

# Fun Discounts for Retirees

*Pensionados* are holders of the permanent resident visa for *Pensioners*. They get the same discounts as Panamanian Retirees on various products and services. Discounts include prescriptions at private pharmacies, meals, public transportation, and plane tickets. To benefit, you must present your *Jubilado* (that means *Retired*) ID card, also known as an *E-Cedula* in Spanish. The "E" denotes foreign (*Foreigner = Extranjero*) residency. *Cedula* means *Identification Card.*

The card's number is like a National ID. Everyone carries it. It is like a Social Security number. Once you get it, it will never change. Keep it with you as you'll have to show it often. And hang on to it. It is easy to lose.

In summary, *Jubilado* sounds like "Who-Bee-Lado," which means *Retired*, and *Pensionado* means *Pensioner*. These terms are interchangeable; don't let that confuse you. You don't need this on your list of frustrations. You will have enough confusing stuff to deal with.

If you have time to burn, get in line and wait like a Panamanian to see a Public Health Doctor. These are the same medical doctors you'll find in private practice. All doctors must serve in Public Health. You should get in line by 6:30 or 6:45 in the morning. You can get routine lab work done at the Public Health Clinic. You can also buy discounted prescription medicine there. If you feel sick in this country, go to the Doctor! *It will not break the bank.* I know I am repeating myself, but it took me years to get that through my thick head.

Private Medical Doctors charge $15-$45 per visit. Private specialists are accessible at a fraction of what I paid back home. Many international retirees have private Panamanian health insurance (about $130/month). They usually go to the Private Hospital called *Hospital Chiriqui* in David.

There is a difference between public and private care. In public care, you may face a long wait for elective procedures. And your recovery usually happens in multi-patient wards. Private hospital rooms are generally for only one to two patients.

**ProTip:** E-Cedula holders get Free Public Health Care! All others pay 50 cents!

Hospital stays in Panama are unique. Family members or friends stay in the patient's room around the clock. Overnight visitors can bring comfort and security. They help the patient, who is their loved one. The overnight person may have to sleep in a warm/hot shared room or a cold private recovery room.

The overnight staying individual may have an uncomfortable oversized reclining sleeper chair. The overnighter may need to bring bedding and supplies for the overnight visit. Being accompanied is a good idea. The companion can protect the patient from medical errors. "Are you sure that's the right medicine?"

It's standard for public and private hospitals not to have certain medications. Someone may need to leave the hospital and buy them. Here's what you do: Go with the prescriptions and the patient's I.D. card. Buy the required medicines from a nearby pharmacy. The nurses usually know where you can find them. If you cannot go, the hospital may be able to refer you to a trusted taxi man who does this.

Chapter 3
# Panama Uses U.S. Dollars

## U.S. Bills are Panama's Balboas

Panama has used U.S. dollars since 1904. The U.S. helped Panama gain independence from Colombia in 1903, and Panama became the Republic of Panama. Yet, not all merchants and banks accept every bill. Taking crisp, new notes with clear, undamaged faces and serial numbers is essential.

Know that stapled, damaged, or defaced bills are hard to spend here. It is usual for Panamanians to refuse old, worn, or torn bills. Act Panamanian and tell them you need a new bill in this situation. Refuse to accept it because you may not be able to spend it!

Also, businesses may refuse older US bills that lack the modern security features in the new $100, $50, or $20 bills. Such bills could be counterfeit. We get many bad bills here. Hence, checking bills before leaving where you got them is crucial. Scrutinize your bills to avoid trouble. Look for watermarks, security threads, and other features. These distinguish US currency from counterfeits. I've seen fake $20 and $50 bills, and they looked real except for those missing security features.

Yes, you need to stay away from old bills. It may be no big deal back home, but here it is. I once had a German guest at my hotel. After I refused to accept his old $50 bill, he confessed he had trouble spending it. He looked distressed. "No one will take it!" I suggested going to a bank, and he did. They lectured him the same. He was grateful they took it off his hands. But they made him sign a document, took a picture of him, asked for his thumbprint, and made a copy of his passport!

Also, nearby countries have coins that look much like US coins. Nicaragua has a coin that looks like a quarter. I once took so many foreign coins that I put out a *free money* jar for our traveling guests. That jar started getting fuller! Everyone was ditching their useless change. Lol! Be careful, and always remember to use caution with cash when traveling abroad.

**ProTip:** Watch your quarters here! Ecuador has a coin that looks like a U.S. Quarter (25-cent piece). They end up in circulation all the time.

## Some Coins Look Different

Coins carrying different art are in circulation. They arrive along with all the typical US bills and coins. Panama has unique versions of 50-cent pieces, quarters, dimes, nickels, and pennies. They have the same color, dimensions, and weight. Spend them before you leave, as these are not legal currencies outside Panama. Or give them to kids or coin collectors. It makes a good story.

Some of those coins are rare. And that makes some of them valuable. I once had a retired guest in my hotel. He explained how he made the money to come down here every six months. He said he sold the rare Panamanian versions of the US coins online. He sold them in complete sets and some as singles. He put some in fancy wood displays. They were so lovely you could hang them on the wall.

Over the years, he had made quite a few Panamanian Bankers friends. He said they never charged him anything. They enjoyed helping him! If I remember correctly, he made at least two dollars per quarter. Some of them are hard for collectors to find. The high-dollar word for the study and collecting of coins is *Numismatics*. It sounds like "noo-miz-ma-ticks." It also sounds like a clever way to pay for your trip here.

These coins exhibit symbols of historical significance and renowned sites. The U.S. Mint creates these unique coins for Panama. Still, you need clarification with some coins. Try to get familiar with them if you can. Don't worry if you get stuck trying to get the correct change. Panamanians are very kind people. Pull out what you have and let the cashier dig through it if you need clarification. I used to do that. So don't freak out. People are happy to help you.

Panamanian coins are the color and size of US coins but signify much more. Depicted on Balboa coins are images of *Vasco Núñez de Balboa*. He was a Spanish explorer. We also have the *Urracá penny* or *Urracá Centesimo*. He was the courageous and celebrated Ngäbe chief. Urracá was a fearsome fighter. He opposed Spanish colonization in the 1520s. His iconic presence on this Panama penny symbolizes resilience and resistance.

No one has conquered this tribe, and it has played a crucial role in uncovering Panama's vibrant history. Urracá united the tribes and inspired them, and the nation is still. In his honor, the Panama Boy Scouts previously awarded the *Scout Urracá*. It was the highest rank for outstanding community service.

The Scouts recently changed the award's name. It is now *Scout Balboa!* I'm looking for a Boy Scout to explain why, because Urrucá beat the Spanish.

# What is a Balboa?

The Balboa is Panama's official currency and is always worth the same as the US Dollar. But this issue often needs clarification because the exchange rate is usually listed!

In Panama, the words U.S. dollar and Balboa mean the same thing. You will see the Balboa sign (B/.) while dining out, shopping, and banking in Panama or the U.S. dollar sign ($). Both symbols are interchangeable and have equal value.

I hear stories about many people who use credit cards or their home banks. They believe that the Balboa does not mean US dollars. The exchange is listed. So they want to charge you for exchanging dollars for balboas! It is laughable, and it can be hard to convince it is not valid. I have had to explain it many times. Being told you must exchange dollars for balboas is a familiar story. *There is no U.S. dollar to the Balboa Exchange!*

In summary, the exchange rate of the Panama Balboa to the United States Dollar is one-to-one. They're equal currencies. You may need help with your credit card company or bank. Even when you warn them, your first transaction here will shut off your debit or credit card. We have a well-marked, free telephone at my hotel's base of the middle staircase. Everyone comes and uses it to call and have their card turned back on.

Converting to Balboas is unnecessary. In Panama, people only use U.S. paper bills ( look cool and call them Balboas). And they accept all U.S. coins. There are no Panamanian bills. Let me repeat myself. There are no legal Balboa bills. Vendors sell them framed so that you can put one on your wall. Visitors will encounter a combination of US coins and the Panamanian Balboa coins.

## The Martinelli Coin

Here is a short story on the Panamanian dollar coin nicknamed the *Martinelli*. Ricardo Martinelli was President of Panama. Following him, the next was President Varela. The next and current one is President Cortizo. President Martinelli mandated the introduction of this coin in Panama. People call this coin a Martinelli. Sometimes, I hear it used for the amount of one dollar. In Panama, it is worth $1. Please note you can only spend these here. They are not legal tender in the States.

It is the only coin similar in design to Canadian coinage, but it is dissimilar to any U.S. coin ever minted. The "Toonie" is the model for it, which is the Bi-Metalic Canadian $2 coin. You won't miss it. It sticks out like a sore thumb in your coin purse. "What the heck is this?" It is silver on the outside and bronze in the middle.

The Martinelli and Varela administrations produced 100 million of these Balboa coins. This set included some commemorative coins using that bimetal model. The mint produced each coin for 30 cents, including transportation to Panama. That is a money-making deal if there ever was one! These coins have a useful life of at least 20 years. They will be around for a while. By comparison, paper dollars last a mere two years.

Panama stopped production in 2019, leaving many oddball coins in circulation. Some commemorate the Roman Catholic Church World

Youth Conference, which the Pope attended in Panama City, Panama. These commemorative coins are also called Martinell's.

In Spanish, they call *World Youth Day 2019*, *Jornada Mundial de la Juventud 2019*. It was the 16th edition of this international event. From January 22-27, youth from across the globe gathered in Panama City, Panama. They had never held an event of such grandeur in Central America. It was a big deal. It represented the Church's dedication to spreading the faith. It also fostered the spirit of fellowship among the younger generations. The country sure had fun!

The Red Cross also has a couple of variations of the Martinelli. Be sure to spend all your Martinellis before you leave Panama. They are not legal currency anywhere else.

## The Panamanian Peso

Does Panama use *Pesos*? That can't be right! Panamanians refer to 50-cent pieces as Pesos. That word, Peso, leads to confusion at the cash register. *Un peso más, Señor,* translates as *One more peso, Sir.* What the heck?

That used to screw me up. It took me years to realize that meant I was 50 cents short. I may be slow, but I can be taught. See? I'm an old dog learning new tricks. What? Are we in Mexico now? That's funny!

*Peso* may refer to half a dollar or a U.S. 50 Cent piece, including the Panamanian version of the 50 Cent piece. Make sure to distinguish it from the *Mexican or Colombian currencies.* Both countries call their currency *Pesos*. Here, it is the nickname given for 50 cents or half a dollar.

As a former teenage student who lived in Mexico City, I found this confusing. When I was there in the '70s, the Mexican one-peso coin was quite similar in size to a US 50-cent piece. Is this where Panamanians got the nickname for it? So, say "peso" for all 50-cent coins. You'll look smart.

**ProTip:** Be Cool! Learn to say, *Plata Blanca.* That's the name people here in Panama call *Coinage.* But understand it. The direct translation to English is *White Silver.* Also, *Un Real* is what they call the *5 Cent Piece* and *Un Pavo (A Turkey)* is used for the *1 Dollar Coin! A Quarter* is often called *Un Cuara!* And *Dies Centavos (10 Cents)* nickname is *Peseta (the currency Spain used until 2002 when they changed to the Euro).*

Chapter 4

# Volunteer Opportunities

In my Rotary Club back in Montana, we did fun volunteer stuff. We took Germans on cattle drives, brandings, and fire parties with barbecue. White Sulphur Springs only had loggers and ranchers for members. Plus, one guy owned the cafe where we met and ate together. On the side, he sold firearms as a licensed gun dealer. Sometimes, in the winter, we only had four members who could show up.

We also gave the kids scholarships and sent them to leadership camp and all that stuff. The Rotary members there were incredible. They were the kind of guys you're happy to cook burgers with for the 4th of July Rodeo every year.

Rotary in Panama has been different. I had to learn the word *Guayabera* and how to wear and buy them. Those classic Latin shirts look so cool on everybody going out to party at a fancy Country Club. The people in the Rotary clubs are full-lifers and seem very professional. I've met many of them; it's like a legacy passed down from grandparents.

And it's such a small crowd here in Panama. They all know each other. I have a cowboy buddy, Amilcar Cerrud Moreno, who was the Honorary Consul to the German Embassy. He is the reason I know so many Germans working and living in Panama. He would bring me German V.I.P.s to stay in my hotel. He now is the head of Chiriqui's German-Panamanian Chamber of Commerce. He is doing a great job, we now celebrate Oktoberfest in Boquete!

During the COVID-19 pandemic, he was the District Governor. He led the Central American and Caribbean Rotary District with new challenges. Zoom calls filled his days. He found solace at their rural retreat with his elegant dancing horse. It was sad he couldn't travel. The new governor's first job is to visit every club in the district. And that is about 60 of them!

Panamanian Rotarians all seem okay. There are some real doers down here. Some friends even started universities, bio-research stations, and nice stuff like that. Panama Rotary is more extensive and better developed than Montana's. We have no cattle drives. But I've upped my game by moving here and joining their Rotary.

# www.Rotary.org

Rotary District #4240

This Rotary Club District covers some interesting territory. It spans Panama, Central America, and El Salvador. It also reaches out to some islands in the Caribbean. Panama is part of District #4240.

*Club Rotario de Boquete* (Rotary Club of Boquete)

- It is the original Rotary Club here in Boquete, Panama. https://sites.google.com/view/clubrotariodeboquete. It is an English-speaking club founded by the David Rotary Club in our provincial capital, David.
- *3 Little Rooms.* This High School at *Salt Creek/Quebrada Sal* is a big deal. It was a first for the Indigenous Community in the Bocas del Toro Province. I surveyed the community. That's when I discovered only six kids had been able to finish high school! I promoted the project. I was the founding chairman of this successful Rotary-sponsored high school project. Now, we have six years of graduates!
- Then, the Boquete Club sponsored a new Bocas del Toro Club!
- *The Manchichi Project - Manchichi* is Ngäbe for Mother and Child. The Boquete Club manages a significant Global Grant from Rotary. The mission is to educate and license Indigenous Midwives in the Comarca Ngäbe-Buglé. They will save mothers and children. Their training and high-tech portable equipment allow them to reach remote, access-challenged areas. These specialists then help them provide early warning for high-risk pregnancies. Dr. Jeffery Flynn

was the chairman and led the project to success. My friend, Dr. Newton Osborn, is a medical doctor in the club. He alarmed us by showing how many mothers and babies were dying. The first group of 27 have graduated. Now, they are starting the next. The Manchichi Project is an internationally acclaimed project that saves Mothers and Children.

Rotary Sunset Club of Boquete

- This second Rotary Club in Boquete, Panama, recently got started. It is Chiriqui Province's second English-speaking club.
- It is a new club formed by people new to Rotary and past Club Rotario de Boquete members. Many newcomers have rushed in.
- Both local clubs burst at the seams, holding energetic members in the 40 - 50 member count range. I expect active membership here in the highlands to top 100 this year. https://rotarysunsetclubofboquete.com

Rotary Eclub One

- This Rotary Club is the first-ever Web-Based Rotary Club worldwide. District 5450 in Colorado, USA, chartered it in 2002. Rotary Eclub One is a very unique club. http://www.rotaryeclubone.org. It has members in over 20 countries, but they are citizens of 27 different countries! This web-based Rotary Club welcomes individuals from anywhere. A total of 75 members make up this diverse club.
- I'm now a member of Rotary Eclub One. I am researching and developing in Panama, running prototype programs, and testing new ideas while doing Community Relations in Indigenous lands. My teams and I coordinate Deployment, Assessment, Data Reporting, and Decision Tree Management.

- My team aims to design a nutrition project that we can *deploy worldwide.* This project's Rotary area of focus is *To Save Mothers and Children.* The design goal is to go beyond sustainability. That would mean its design is so productive that it self-replicates and spreads.
- The current project prototype has three design components.
- The first is *Moringa Trees.* In Africa, people know them as *The Miracle Tree.* They are the most nutritious plant on earth and a good fertilizer.
- The second part is *Rabbit Husbandry.* Four Rabbits in four years can produce 4 million! They could feed the world, and their poop and pee are excellent fertilizers.
- The third component comes from the methods taught by *Foundations for Farming.* https://foundationsforfarming.org/. This food-growing system is bio-intensive farming (8 times more food/area used). Their process can be organic with heirloom seeds at zero costs. Methods include seed banking, natural pest control, and rapid hot compost production.
- I became a Foundations for Farming Certified Instructor Trainer two years ago. I trained in a beautiful area. It was lakeside on the borderlands of the *Emberá and Guna Yala Tribes of Panama.* Lots of crocodiles! No, I didn't go swimming like the others! But I did end up face-to-face with a three-and-a-half footer. He jumped onto the foredeck of my kayak! I couldn't tell who was more freaked out, him or me. Our Ngäbe Partnership gave me a scholarship for that training, and I felt very honored.
- I invite you to join us. I am seeking funding and volunteers for this project. You don't have to be a member, but I need your help.

Who We Are

- *Worldwide,* Rotary is a *Network* of 1.4 million people. We are neighbors, friends, leaders, and problem solvers who envision a world where people *Unite* and take *Action* to make *Lasting Change* around the *Globe*, in our *Communities*, and *Ourselves*."

- For more inspiring information on Rotary - www.Rotary.org.

What Does Rotary Do?

Rotary members believe in taking responsibility for tackling ongoing global challenges together.

Over 46,000 clubs working together for these seven causes:

- Fighting Disease
- Growing Local Economies
- Promoting Peace
- Providing Clean Water
- Saving Mothers & Children
- Supporting Education
- Protecting the Environment

# Amigos de los Animales and Boquete Dog Camp

Let me tell you about *Amigos de los Animales, Animal Friends.* They are a great group. They offer free monthly pet care instruction and check-ups as well as spaying and neutering for cats and dogs. They provide excellent service, education, and treatments.

They have a fantastic team of volunteers who care for the animals and help them find forever homes. The facility is clean and inviting, and the staff welcomes you to learn more about their work.

Their facility in Alto Boquete is impressive! It is large and spotless, and its teams of volunteers are outstanding. Ruby, the director, is my friend. She's been so helpful. She loaned us pet carriers for trips into the Indigenous Territories. We needed them for the Rabbits part of our work. She's the best, and I am not the only one here saying it!

The Amigos de los Animales Volunteers are a happy crowd. They enjoy pursuing their education and direct community service goals.

They work well together and get stuff done. They have a large group of volunteers and a large crowd when they are running clinics.

There's also a new and fast-growing destination for volunteering. You can work with our furry friends at *Boquete Dog Camp!* Not only is that going on, but I know Boquete has a cat rescue/sanctuary for our feline friends.

So, when you get to Boquete, you can check out Amigos de los Animales, Boquete Dog Camp, and the Cat Sanctuary. And guess what? Someone told me there's even a group that rescues horses. I'm impressed by the incredible strides made here to help animals and their owners.

By the way, I'm a cowboy and must say that Boquete has the finest riders and the most incredible horses I have ever seen. The *Cabalgatas*, or *Horse Parades*, are lovely spectacles. The biggest is in David, which has over 9000 horses! The beautiful horses, tack, and riders are a spectacle. The whole population attends these parades. Get the disco balls out of storage because the *Dancing Horses* are here! I've never seen anything like that back at the ranch!

I have one more animal group to mention. There is a dog training group I see around town. The fact is, we've got a bunch of good dog trainers here. How awesome is witnessing a parade of rescued and pedigreed dogs line up with their owners? They move together in sync in Boquete's *Parque Central* (*Central Park*). You know the move. Every step of the line of owners, damn dogs jump through between their legs. The dogs synchronize with their steps.

## Boquete Health and Hospice

I adore these folks! They exude professionalism and order in all that they do. They've grown a lot, and I need help keeping track of their fantastic work. Please review their broad work areas at https://www.boquetehospice.org/.

They loan out items, including the usual stuff needed for the bedridden. They also have hospital beds and oxygen generators for those in need. Many have donated to increase their inventory. Those oxygen generators are not that expensive, and they improve lives.

Additionally, they played a crucial role in establishing the blood bank. Many of the group's members have expertise in relevant fields. Thanks to their tireless efforts, we now have a blood bank in Chiriqui Province. Families in crises used to go on Facebook begging for blood donors!

They train certified volunteers in groups. Many of their members did this or similar work before retirement, but not all members did. I know plenty of people who got their first training and certification through them, and I can see how rewarding it is for them.

They also have some bedside toilets, crutches, and wheelchairs to lend. Boquete Health and Hospice offers many educational programs and health screenings. You can see them weekly. They take blood pressure and educate at the Tuesday Market from 9 a.m. to 12 noon. It's at the lower river bridge in Bajo Boquete.

They are our most mission-driven, serious volunteer service group. They have been meeting at my hotel, Hotel Central Boquete, so I know many of the members and leaders. It is a harmonious, hard-working, and productive group. Like them, I, too, have strong feelings about hospice. Both my parents passed with dignity while in hospice care.

## Basura Busters

Have you heard of the group called *Basura Busters (*or *Trash Busters*)? Some of my local expat friends created it. This volunteer group includes a retired couple from the United States. They are long-distance runners. I know her well since she's part of a close-knit hiking crew of friendly ladies. They often swing by my coffee shop after their walks. Her husband is a retired U.S. Marine officer. I like them!

It makes me so proud to see them out serving the community. It's all about busting the garbage! They go all decked out in bright green shirts and gloves. Every Sunday, they set out on cleanup missions.

They're all geared up with those big garbage bags and those long grabber thingies. They go through different neighborhoods.

The cherry on top? They make new friends, often eating together. That's how they show how much they care about Boquete. And I've noticed they've inspired the locals! They're starting to do the same on their own on random days. If you're interested, they are happy to accept new volunteers. This volunteer mission provides a great chance to make new connections. It also lets you help a worthy cause.

Chapter 5
# Organic Food

## Direct from your Favorite Farmer

Why not chat with your friends and neighbors? See if they're already getting deliveries from an organic farm or gardener. The inside info you can get might surprise you. It's a wallet-friendly way to score hard-to-find organic goodies. You might discover your neighbors are farmers. They might give you their extra avocados, oranges, plantains, tomatoes, and bananas. Or sell them at unbeatable prices!

We have a great guy who brings fresh fish from the coast daily. He has a specific route and parks in different neighborhoods at different times. Look for the pickup truck he comes up in. He has colossal ice chests full of fresh seafood in the back. He has a large scale to weigh out the fish. It hangs from the box's rack in the back. I love his tuna steaks, pan-fried in butter. They are sushi-grade!

I know people who get a big bag of organic oranges every week. They are inexpensive and a bit ugly but don't worry about that. In the morning, indulge in fresh-squeezed orange juice. There are so many new organic operations under greenhouses that it takes work to keep up.

I love goat cheese and avocado toast! Many of my friends here are crazy for avocado toast as well. This town consumes a lot of avocados and goat cheese. We have a goat farm tour to see where that cheese comes from. There's nothing cuter than baby goats. So, ask around. There are quite a few new places now serving avocado toast with goat cheese. It is available in organic form and sourced from our community.

## The Orgánica Store

I recently discovered this store at the new *Los Senderos Mall* in Bajo Boquete. *Los Senderos* means *The Trails*. It is impressive! If you eat

Vegan, they have that, not only organic. They have vegan snacks, cheese, milk, and ice cream. They carry the *Just Egg* and *Beyond Meat* products and sell gluten-free flour and breads. They have a wide variety of organic groceries.

They also have great toiletries/personal care, home, and cleaning products. It's stuff that's okay for *chemically sensitive people*. Seeing the large variety for such a small town shocked me. In many ways, Boquete is the perfect place. You can escape environmental chemicals and toxins.

They have products for pets, babies, and children and bulk items sold out of clean and tidy bins. They sure have a lot packed into such a small store. They also have helpful, friendly, bilingual staff.

They have organic supplements. They told me they could likely get what you need if they didn't have it. Talk to them if you are searching for a specific product you use and would like to be able to buy it here in town. I am a fan of *Mycology*, the science of mushrooms. They have an excellent selection of organic mushroom supplements. That is where I buy my *Agarikon Mushroom* and *Turkey-Tail Mushroom* supplements. I would like to support them while avoiding shipping costs from the States.

## Boquete Bulk Organics Buying Club

Jane Moodie runs the *BOBC* (*Boquete Bulk Organics Buying Club*). The lifetime membership is only $10. Please look at their website. Sign up for their fabulous Newsletter at https://boquetebobc.com.

Coconut Products operates under their roof. They sell coconut oil, water, cream, pulp, flour, butter, and grated coconut.

Send her an email by 2 p.m. Sunday for Coconut Products. That is when the husking starts. They cold press premier coconut oil from wild-harvested, Panamanian island-grown coconuts. That means they are fresh and delicious. You can smell it coming from a mile away.

Their equipment is stainless steel. Their products are pure coconut and only coconut. "We make the products fresh and then dispense them directly into your containers." The BOBC's online ordering system takes orders for the Coconut Products business.

The BOBC is a club with benefits. Their pantry is a backup storage space, and their extra storage is for those who need more room for all their bulk food. They have limited storage. Community Pantry Hours: Monday and Thursday 12-16, Tuesday 11-5, and Friday 10-5. The store closes on Wednesday, Saturday, and Sunday. They want me to remind you to bring your containers.

They also let you pick up pork product orders at BOBC from *Casa de Cerdo* down in David. Here is a lovely testimonial. "They're a small, high-quality shop, conscientious of the animals they oversee and their customers. They have organized their shop with a variety of selections for customers to choose from."

Quite a few folks here say that Casa de Cerdo products and their shop in David are impressive. It has a pin on Google Maps to help you find it. You can speak to Juan Carlos in English at +507-6261-9774 (WhatsApp). Jane keeps only a sample of their work, which you can see at her shop.

## Tuesday Morning Farmers Market

When I arrived over a decade ago, the *Tuesday* or *Gringo Market* was no big deal. But it sure is now! Some people are sensitive to the word gringo and call it the *Tuesday Market*. I don't think that word carries the stigma it used to. Now it means US citizen.

And it's not only Gringos there. Now, it looks like the lobby of the *United Nations*. It starts at 9 a.m. and ends at midday. At high noon, a loud air horn is the alert to get-er-done. The far or east side of the Bajo Boquete bridge is where you can find this once-a-week market. It crosses over the main river, *Rio Caldera*.

It was only on the right side (south), at the *B.C.P.* (Boquete Community Players). *The Tap-Out* sports bar rents space there now. You must see their sign from the bridge. When you arrive on the far side, it is on your right. But now that farmer's market has grown. It's on the right and left (S.E. corner of the *Boquete Flower Fair*).

Two separate markets are happening on the same day. One is at one location, the other at another. Different people organize them. It's two Tuesday markets for the price of one. And yes, they are both still *Free!*

> **ProTip:** Experience trading with the region's Indigenous people. They live in Boquete and sell their goods at the Tuesday Morning Market:

Ngäbe Tribe

1. *Chácara* Bags - These are the country's iconic *everyday carry-over-the-shoulder bags*. *Kra* is an ultralight, ultra-rugged natural plant fiber used in Chácara. It is almost impossible to wear traditional ones out. They are over-the-shoulder bags that both men and women carry. New designs in modern materials are also available. I prefer the traditional.
2. *Naguas* - These are colorful trade-cloth dresses for women and girls of the Ngäbe people of Panama. Boquete is a border town on the west side of their lands. You'll see those lovely dresses everywhere. Other items are handmade traditional hats, bracelets, and necklaces that are very beautiful. These are essential sources of income for their families.

Guna Yala Tribe

1. *Molas* - People from the far reaches of Panama recognize them as renowned fabric art pieces. They hold a special place in the hearts of the Guna Yala people of Panama. No longer known as San Blas, the government of Panama has honored the Tribe's request for a name change. In the Guna language, *Dulegaya*, the word *mola* means *cloth and clothing*. People use the phrase mola to refer to artistic

45

panels and complete blouses. These garments, crafted from imported materials, are unique. Each is a one-of-a-kind design and construction.

Using the reverse appliqué technique, they adorn the panels with intricate designs. This technique involves temporarily stitching together layers of differently colored cotton fabric. Then, with great attention to detail, the top layer is carefully cut to reveal the layers below. This method creates a visually captivating display of vibrant colors. Cut edges are carefully folded and sewn to enhance their beauty.

You can roll up your molas for transport. They are perfect for framing and displaying in your home. My sister has a beautiful one on her wall! If you're seeking authentic molas, look no further than my Guna friends, *Laro* and *Lopez*. They have a diverse selection, ranging from traditional to transitional and modern molas.

Some molas may hold significant value. The traditional designs appear reminiscent of movie monsters—two-headed crocodiles and worse. The traditional designs are one of a kind. They come from the dreams of the talented ladies who bring them to life.

I encourage you to get to know these incredible individuals. They have some excellent deals. I once met some Germans who mentioned a shop in Berlin, Germany. They have exquisitely framed molas that sell for hundreds and thousands of dollars each.

Peruvian Indigenous

1. *Alpaca*—It is a luxury fiber sold here at discount prices. Peruvian Indigenous producers (the ancestors of the Incas) sell it here in blankets, ponchos, and jackets. The scarves are divine. Woven alpaca is water-resistant and breathable. It is hard to wear out garments made of alpaca. The fiber is remarkably resilient.
2. *Moonstone*—This semi-precious stone is the mystical gemstone associated with June. My Peruvian Indigenous friends always have the best. Ask for them by name. The mother's name is *Calista Illanacanchi*. Her son is *Nelson*

*Anothon Mamani* and her daughter is *Marina Michael Mamani*. One of them will surely be there. Take a look at these premium quality vibrant blue stones. These emit a mesmerizing orange glow in the light. Those same Germans have explained how rare they are.

Where do you go? They've given the Indigenous front-row seats in the original farmers market on the right or south side. They're right at the bottom of the entry stairs, making finding them easy.

These two marketplaces offer an incredible array of goods. Enjoy purchasing coffee from local farmers. In the new market (the North side), they take turns serving the world's finest brew. They offer free cups. The sheer excellence of their coffee alone makes this market an absolute must-try!

The markets have a great variety. There's a guy sharpening knives and scissors. Individuals are offering second-hand books for sale. You can buy authentic chocolate crafted with high cacao levels. It delivers the benefits of a superfood.

The Rotary Club, a Chiropractor, and a Massage Therapist have booths, and every other volunteer group has one. You can buy jewelry from the artist there as well. There are usually gold and silver brokers, both buying and selling.

There used to be only one or two people selling organic food, but now many small local producers exist. Get there early. Many organic farmers sell out by 10 a.m. It's an excellent place to meet members of the community and people-watch.

The market run at the BCP (where the *TapOut* bar & grill is) sometimes has live music on its stage in the back, by the river. Sometimes, there's singing. I like to hang out under the shade tree near the stage to chat with new and old friends.

> **ProTip:** Make new friends. The market north of the intersection usually has free local coffee. It also has a lovely outdoor space where you can sit around a table in the shade or sun with people.

Pass through the market to the bathrooms. You will see the small patio they fenced off to steal some of the flower fair territory.

After you buy your Organic Food, notice the fantastic selection of fresh street food. Some families are there selling fruit wines, organic and not, from their farms in the hills. You have unlimited jewelry and vitamins to choose from. Plus, there is a farm fresh strawberry kiosk across the street! The Tuesday Morning Market is a great place to chat and hang out.

## Thursday Morning Farmers Market

This is very new and big! It runs from 9:00 a.m. to 12:00 noon Thursday mornings in Alto Boquete, Panama. There is a much larger selection of produce there than the other market places on Tuesday morning. You will find homemade foods, crafts from local artisans, and baked goods (Including gluten-free). It is easy to find. Just search for the Amigos de Animales building. That is where it is held. Here is a link to take a tour while learning about our fruits, vegetables and the market:
https://calendar.boquete.app/event/farmers-market-guided-tour-15/

Chapter 6
# Multicultural Community

## Diversity Living As One

We went through the backdoor, like Rick Steves's (Guide Books to Europe) *"Through the Backdoor."* When I arrived in Boquete, *Don Plinio Ruiz* was Panama's greatest living coffee baron. People put *Don* for men and *Doña* for women at the front of the names of the most respected individuals. He was in his early 90s. He introduced me to this diverse community.

He was famous in two ways: as a *Comerciante (Businessman)* and a *Delegado Electoral (Election Delegate)*. First, he founded *Café Ruiz—Excellence in Coffee as a businessman.* He joinedthe leaders of Boquete's transformation to *Specialty Coffee.* That is coffee scoring 80 points or above judged on the 100-point scale of the *Specialty Coffee Association Cupping Form.* The second was from his service to Panama to keep Democracy respected every five years during elections.

He was Panama's longest-serving electoral delegate. His special front license plate showed his authority and responsibility over voting. In gratitude, the Republic of Panama gave him a chest full of gold medals.

Every Presidential candidate made it a point to meet him first. They needed his blessing. I relished hearing his thoughts on where he would sit with them. It would be in the glassed back of my hotel. It has a great view. I'd serve them from the coffee shop, of course, while he sips *his* delicious brew. That part of his *Vision Quest* came true. His daughter, Dr Maria Ruiz (double PhD and a Master's Degree!), still makes our coffee. She is one of the world's most excellent coffee experts.

## My Guide

He taught me much that guided my development as a Boqueteno. He was a wise mentor. He taught me to avoid controversy and get along with everyone. As an election delegate, he had to stay neutral in public on all things controversial or political. As a businessman, he showed me the importance of keeping friendly relations with everyone. He opened all the doors to me.

The origin story of our friendship is a good one. Nearly 12 years back, soon after I arrived, Don Plinio shared that he saw himself as the luckiest man alive. I arrived in Boquete soon after he had a "little situation." Yeah, his heart stopped while driving. Then he crashed into the ditch and hit his chest on the steering wheel; that blow restarted his heart. Lucky. Pretty dang lucky. Except for the part about the medical procedure for removing his driver's license,

When we met, he was a happy new owner of a new pacemaker/ defibrillator implanted in his chest. He was already in his 90s, but his heartbeat sang loud and strong. He had a great attitude about life. I liked his coffee and his coffee shop. So I often visited. He lived next door to the café, so we soon got acquainted. He was a dapper gentleman in a short-brim, feather-trimmed fedora, hat, and suit. He had charisma, friends everywhere, and *no license to drive*.

He was an eagle-eyed observer of people. He studied me. Wearing his best dubious face, he asked, "So you're telling me you're some kind of cowboy dentist?" I told him, "Yes, I finished a guided Implant and Prosthetic Surgery Residency in Utah."

That did not interest him one bit. "But you're a *real* cowboy? He pointed up to the continental divide. "You can drive a 4x4 in a place like that?". I said, "Sure." He looked unconvinced. "You don't scare easily, do you?" "No, not too much. I'm used to driving steep, slippery Montana mountains with a load of cattle or horses behind." That made him smile.

## The Coffee King

He stood up and said, "Well, let's see about that!" He tossed me his keys, and off we went. I could not have had more fun or met more people had I been driving the President of Panama around. Folks thought I was his long-lost son or something. It was a great comedy that he presented me as some sort of foreign dignitary.

I was a nobody sitting next to *The King of Coffee*. I drove him around town and then up into his Eden-like highland farms. He loved teaching me and sharing the bounty from one-of-a-kind fruit trees hidden away. We would go to the end of crazy two-track trails, climbing to the surrounding wilderness in his new 4x4. We had so much fun.

That is how I met untold numbers of people from the Boquete community. He introduced me to fascinating Indigenous, Panamanians, and Expats. We would talk with millionaires and billionaires. He put me in front of people from every class, race, religion, or economic status. And he treated all with equal respect and dignity. He believed it created a better community by helping people like me improve. He cared about people's souls and their development.

He was an excellent salesman, having learned from his very entrepreneurial mother. His daughter, Dr. Maria Ruiz, my adopted sister, told me a good story. When he was a kid, his mom would send him downtown to the train station to sell flowers. I got to tell her dad's story. One day, with her father in the high country, he showed me a secret spot in a hidden valley. That's where he and his brother picked those wildflowers they sold as boys.

Even far above that spot, he had friends. We once went to the end of the road on a steep-sided ridge. He surprised me with his sharp tone, "Doc! We are goners if you drive off that ledge! Creep out there and park close so we can let the engine cool and catch the view."

He didn't want to die, nor did I! I did as he said and crept out till he barked, "Whoa!" We sat silent, listening to the hot engine's ding and howler monkeys' echoes. It was an outstanding moment and a hell of a view of one of his farms.

He said, "Listen!" I replied, "To what?" He shushed me and said, "I hear someone coming." I heard it, too, someone climbing up to us, stopping every couple of steps to swing a machete. He jumped out. "Come on, Timmy!"

51

Out of the jungle's edge of that cliff comes a guy Don Plinio had known since he was a boy. He looked to be in his late 80s. He held an extra-long machete almost as old as he was. I saw a new file sticking out of his belt. He'd sharpened it so much that it was nearly as skinny as a pirate's sword.

Carried across the shoulder with a red cord was a colorful traditional Spanish bota bag (typically carrying wine). A tiny fanny pack was fastened at his waist. I asked him what he was drinking. He said he only had drinking water. I looked down at the hill while they debated the guy's age. Damn! It was steep! He climbed it while trimming and cleaning Don Plinio's coffee! They happily chattered like boys in the schoolyard. Then he turned around, headed down, choppin' away.

Don Plinio laughed and said, "I am sure he's wrong. He can't be 82. He must be around 88 or 89 years old. But at his age, it is okay to lose track." He pointed out his house far, far below. I am pretty sure there's something in the water here. Boquete is a *Blue Zone* where happy, strong, active old folks live.

## The Elders

He would say, "Timmy, drive us over to see *The Elders*." He enjoyed visiting *Belgica's* (my friend and retired first hotel employee) house. She worked most of her life for Don Plinio. He'd trained her in coffee, given her first job. I soon discovered he wanted me to hire her for my new hotel. Her family had three or four over 100 years old back then!

He loved to take his suit coat and get on his knees to fight with their big dog. "Stop Plinio! He's going to bite you!" He kept the dog snapping his teeth right where his hand had been. One of the elderly ladies leaned over and whispered in my ear, "He's never going to change. He's been putting these dog fights on this since he was a little boy. He's a rascal!" Then she giggled.

He enjoyed his customers at his coffee shop. He would tell jokes and do magic tricks for the ladies and children. Then he would challenge men to arm wrestling! He sure was something. I once recorded him showing off his childhood skills to a terrified audience. He was toying with a big scary bug called *Mata Caballo*, the *Horse Killer*. And yes, it does!

## Learn or Teach Spanish, English, or Any Language

You'll love the language learning opportunities in Boquete, a backwater full of a mix of cultures and languages from around the world. Here, we share sweet and serendipitous encounters with people from different countries. And it's pretty darn impressive!

Consider Linda and Joe, a retired couple living as expats. They devoted years to loving and guiding a young girl towards English fluency. Every time they came to my coffee shop at the hotel, we were all so proud to hear her speak. Moments like these make Boquete an extraordinary place!

I have Korean friends who live here who broker coffee. Their wonderful daughter has been a lifelong friend since before she was walking. She calls me *The Egg-Man* because she likes how I make her breakfast egg. They are wonderful people. Many Koreans live here. They include the Baptist preacher (Timoteo) at First Baptist Church, next to the hotel.

> **Pro Tip:** People call individuals with the same name *Tocayos* (*Namesakes*). Timoteo is my name in Spanish. So, my Baptist preacher friend and I have the same name. We are Tocayos! And they refer to us as such. That is a great word to know and use.

We once had a Romanian chess master who came from Canada. People come from everywhere. They say this is the best place to live in the world—and that does not count what our tourists say.

## Backpackers

We get all kinds of tourists here. The largest group among them are *Adventure Travelers*. They look like backpackers. You'll see them on their way to Boquete. They carry enormous expedition-size packs on their backs and often have a half-size pack in the front! I watch them arrive every day, packed into public buses. They are grinning ear to ear. Take a walk through Central Park, and you'll spot them. They are merrily exploring the area, carrying all their gear on their backs.

The Bajo Boquete Central Park (with the fountain and clock) looks like the lobby of the United Nations. I caught a German friend learning French from another friend I didn't know spoke French! I said, "What are you guys doing?" The German said, "I have time now, so I've decided to finish learning French!"

You know what? I know about 20 people trading English classes for Spanish with locals. It's pretty cool! Most Panamanian parents and elders encourage English fluency. Being bilingual is terrific! It opens up so many doors to incredible opportunities. I am generous with my time and patience. I like to help folks who want to practice their English. It's easy to find opportunities here to practice language skills or phrases. You can practice them in many different languages. It can be fun to help others that way.

I was waiting anxiously to meet *Ali*. He is the older brother of my local Palestinian-Jordanian-Colombian-Panamanian friend *Ayed (sounds like Ajed)*. We are old friends. He owns the *Gigante* and *Mräga* (Arabic for *Family*) stores downtown. This brother is brilliant. As a boy in a refugee camp for Palestinians in Jordan, he got the top score on testing and won a full-ride scholarship to Bergen, Norway.

He is the legacy of a 600-year relationship between the Vikings and Arabs! The Vikings had attacked Alhambra, ransacking and killing almost everyone. It was the peaceful preserver of knowledge in the Middle Ages. The Vikings returned to strike a few years later but were ready for them. They had great warriors, too. They let a few Vikings live and sent them home with an Arabic treaty, trade, and knowledge delegation.

This ancient trade relationship is why we still see Arabs who are white, freckled, red-haired, green, or blue-eyed. The Vikings would stop on the way to steal and enslave beautiful women from the British Isles to trade with them. I knew nothing about all this until I got to meet him. He is now a freshly retired professor from Bergen, Norway! That is where my mother's *Viking* roots are from. He spent his life there.

Ali is quite the linguist. He speaks our people's local language, *Old Norwegian!* From him, I learned that my mom's name, *Ila,* means *Moose(female)!* What a rich life we have here. I often drink coffee over long chats with my Arab friends at Buckle Tip.

A young Hasidic Rabbi from Venezuela moved here a few years ago. His family stayed in the hotel, and he and his wife were my neighbors. We have become good friends. He had a few challenging years during the COVID-19 Pandemic. We all did. I'm proud of him. He's constructing a new Synagogue in Bajo Boquete. He also has a Kosher Bakery/Coffee shop called *Morton's Bakehouse.* I like his dad. He's also a Rabbi.

My parents taught me to love and accept people of all faiths as a child. My dad was a Lutheran Hospital Chaplain. He worked with the traveling Rabbi and Catholic Bishop. He would often bring those two to our house for supper. They were far from home. Both covered the large territory of the Dakotas. I have great memories of that funny Rabbi. He made me feel special, sometimes letting me sit on his knee and telling me stories.

**Pro Tip:** *Mitakuye Oyasin!* Learn from the Lakota. Mitakuye Oyasin means *All My Relations. We are All Related.* You say it to petition God on behalf of everything and everyone on Mother Earth. Mitakuye Oyasin affirms the sacredness of life, including humans, animals, plants, and all living things. It also honors each person's spiritual path.

How can they call in the Eagles? I love the elder's story. "It was a mighty battle; we had won the war. The poor, pitiful, two-leggeds had joined forces with the winged. We fought side by side to steal creation from those who ruled over us (the four-legged). The winged ones flew up and took the Blue-Robed Father (the sky). We claimed and were made responsible for the Green Robed Mother (the earth).

It is so." I say, "Aooh! Mitakuye Oyasin! To all my Relàtions! A-ho!"

# We Get Along Here

*"Can't we all just get along?"* That's my favorite quote from *Newman Washington* (my Indian Brother). Those are some excellent, wise words. Aren't we grown-ups responsible for caring for and protecting kids and elders? Shouldn't they come first? They sure do in this town.

Kids come first at our library. Talk to the staff. They are friendly folks. You can get a library card with a utility bill or a rental contract. Sometimes, the Boquete Library gives free English and Spanish lessons.

I am figuring out the process for volunteering to teach. Talk to the director. But I have a gringo friend who teaches *Chess* to kids there. He now leads a team of the best ones in big-time competitions!

Search: "Spanish School + Boquete" on Google for more comprehensive Spanish programs. You will find many local schools and private-teacher options. I know of several private Spanish instructors who tutor people here and online. That's great for people who travel a lot or visit back to their home countries. Don't skip your lessons.

Search online. Panama has programs where you can stay and study in many locations. Get to know the country. You live and learn in a variety of areas. It may be the best of all possible worlds. That way, you can learn Spanish in the mountains and at the beach.

People of all ages come to Boquete to learn Spanish. You will see them doing homework in our parks and coffee shops. Some enjoy group settings, while others prefer private or small group classes. Get custom-tailored to your preferences.

Do you have a burning desire to learn Spanish? Boquete can help you achieve your goal. It doesn't matter whether you stay for one month or six. I am very proud of my nephew Levi. He is my sister's youngest child. We have been close all his life.

He came down and spent his last free High School summer here. He is now in college and pretty fluent. He was very determined when he returned to Iowa. He kept up with it. He practiced speaking Spanish daily with a fellow High School kid from Guatemala.

## She Conquered Spanish

I have a friend who learned Spanish with the *Post-It-Note* method. I had to laugh when I walked into her home. She'd stuck hundreds of colorful notes on everything, folded over, hiding the Spanish translation of the English word in front. That is clever. She was so determined. Everything in her house had a Post-It-Note stuck to it.

I overheard her speaking Spanish in a crowd a year or two later. I recognized the voice, but it surprised me that she spoke Spanish. Good job, *Helena!*

Spanish is a *very doable* skill to pick up here. It will open up a new world, and you will never regret the work or the rewards.

**ProTip:** *Duolingo* is Free at the Apple or Google Play stores. https://en.duolingo.com/. It is a downloadable language-learning app for almost any language, including Spanish. Researchers have based it on studies of how the brain learns. You see one, then say one. You read one, then you write one. And it remembers what you forget. Get started today! You can do it.

I recommend you give Spanish Duolingo at least 15 minutes per day. It's the easiest and fastest way to learn beginner's survival Spanish. So, download it now. Start tomorrow morning with coffee and Duolingo—your daily Spanish class.

You practice the new stuff at the local market and coffee shops. It is easy to practice your new skills here. The locals are amiable and patient. So don't forget your list of new words and phrases. Copy and carry them in your pocket. The stress of using them burns them into your memory! Be patient with yourself. A little daily effort will get you a long way.

Use it or lose it! Errors are part of the fun. Strive harder by embracing a few mistakes along the way. Use what you learn immediately. Then you'll be talking. *Anyone* can learn Spanish. Keep updating that list in your pocket. Write down and focus on your most challenging words and phrases. That is what I did. Patience and consistency are the key ingredients for success on your language journey.

**ProTip:** *Google Translate + Your Smartphone = Language, Learning Magic!*

Take pictures of all the signs you see in Spanish during your typical day here. Then, run those pictures through Google Translate. Next, jot down those words on your new vocabulary list. This list will allow you to review (and learn) those words when you walk by those signs!

**Pro Tip:** Try theDefense Language Institute F.O.R.T.E. method to learn Spanish. Write a paragraph about: 1. Family 2. Occupation 3. Recreation 4. Travel 5. Education.

# The Switzerland of the Americas

Long ago, many Swiss families settled here. They may have started calling Panama the *Switzerland of the Americas.* Some of the older buildings and homes have a Swiss style of architecture. They were some of the first outsiders to come to the valley, which looks like the mountainous green valleys of Switzerland. They liked the weather, the black volcanic soil, and the ability to grow food here all year round.

Both are small, neutral countries with small populations. And we're both peaceful places. We don't draft kids and send them off to war. We get along with everybody. No one cares about who you love or marry. Acceptance is the key to their serenity. They enjoy the gay marching band majorettes. They don't bat an eye when two people of different races get together.

But Panamanians describe people with words that used to shock me. I'm still not comfortable repeating them. They don't say them in a mean way—not at all! They describe people by their appearance! Prepare yourself. They can be pretty graphic and sort of hilarious at the same time. I've had to adjust my thinking and check my personal bias.

# Oops!

I have a friend here, and I love him like a good big brother. The locals call him *Gordo (Fat)*. But not to his face, like I once did. That would be disrespectful. Yeah, he's a big guy. A Latino Panamanian family calls the black guy who married into the family *Carbóncito (Charcoal)*. But not to his face, either. That means charcoal. The -cito at the end indicates they love him.

The kid with noticeable Asian eyes—yep, they call him *Chino (Chinese)*. That one is straight up, out in the open. Go figure. I can't do the math. I'm not from Panama and don't know what's acceptable here. Don't freak out about how they celebrate Black Ethnicity Month in the schools! Panama is its little world with its own rules, I guess.

They call electronic stores and small grocery stores *Chinos*. Four percent of Panamanians are of Chinese descent, and they dominate those business categories. I was invited to join a Chinese Panamanian business support and investment group that is now open to everyone.

I could go on and on. When I first arrived, I thought it was strange to identify people and places that way—sort of shocking. Now, it seems charming and very, very Panamanian. Panama is an open-minded and multicultural country. Remember, it's a vibrant center for trade between the East and West.

Are you married? Are you moving here with a reluctant spouse? Here is a warning from Don Plinio Ruiz. (God Rest His Soul) These are his wise words about the real risks to newcomers' marriages. And yes, he was teasing me about my first wife.

**ProTip:** "Timmy, they come in *Pairs*, but they leave in *Singles*!"

While saying it, he would laugh and dance two fingers across his palm, then back, bouncing with only one. Yes, he was talking about how common it is for newcomer couples to divorce after arrival! I bet you wonder why. Here's a generic example to contemplate.

The guy has worked his tail off his whole life. He has a burning desire to move here and dreams of going deep-sea fishing full-time. But the wife can only live with having her kids and grandchildren nearby. Both are trying to make the other one happy. That's a recipe for disaster. I've often seen that path lead to ruin.

Chapter 7
# Easy Airport Access

## Boquete to David Airport by Taxi

Are you planning to travel from Boquete to Enrique Malek Airport (DAV) in David by taxi? Hold on to your hat—there's a hack to master!

The cab costs range from $25 to $45, which is alright. But, if you plan to leave before sunrise, brace yourself to pay more to ensure a trustworthy ride.

Many people have a meltdown at my hotel. When their taxi driver fails to arrive on time, risking them missing their flight. It's about more than showing up on time, isn't it? You don't want to worry. You need someone reliable and responsible.

My tip is to avoid looking for a better deal downtown at the last minute. Stick to the church boys who know their way around town. They are serious about their jobs and reputation. It's worth $35-$45. Buyer beware!

Here's the story about one of those *Church-Boy* kind of guys. His name is *Gonzalo*. He has a nice, clean, yellow, four-door pickup truck. He's a no-hangover-on-Monday kind of fellow. He comes early. He likes to chat with me and drink our famous coffee. Call my hotel, and we will hook you up. We know who the good ones are.

Two other new options in Chiriqui Province are *Indrive* and *Uber*. Both use downloadable apps. Indrive is different from Uber. Uber has fixed pricing, but Indrive allows you to bid or offer a price. If the driver wants to do it at the rate you are offering, they click ok, and you get picked up and transported at that price.

I used Uber in Panama City, and it was great. However, they only allow vehicles up to two years old. I don't know about local availability for either service, as I have zero experience with them in this province. You will have to check it out yourself when you get here.

It's good to have friends with cars. Slip them a couple of bills to get to David's airport early. Go early. Indulge in a moment of relaxation. Savor a delightful cup of Boquete coffee served by the two coffee shops inside.

David Airport has good, Free WiFi. So does Tocumen, the Panama City International Airport. That will keep you entertained online while you wait. Go through security early to skip the stress of the last-minute line-up. There will be one line only.

The secure waiting areas have plenty of electrical plug-ins. They're far from the chairs. So, I carry a skinny ten-foot extension cord to top up my electronic device's charge while using them. Past the security check, you'll find good bathrooms and air conditioning.

> **ProTip:** *Copa Airlines* flies in and out of Tocumin International Airport (PTY). It is in Panama City, Panama. https://www.copaair.com. Air Panama does not go there. https://www.airpanama.com. It flies into Albrook International Airport (PAC) across the city. A taxi between them costs $23-$28 and takes 21 minutes on a good day. And not every day is a good one over there. Traffic can get crazy, and you might miss your connection.

## Boquete to David Airport by Bus + Taxi

Many retirees like adventure. Or are they trying to pinch pennies? They want to go to David Airport by public bus. The confusion starts when they search for the bus that goes to the airport. There is none. You must take a taxi from the David bus terminal to the airport. The Airport is out on the east side of the city of David.

Here's another piece of that puzzle. I worry if you are on the bus going down during rush hour. The bus might be standing room only, with employees heading to work. That bus will make many stops to pick people up and let them off. It might take you over an hour to get to the bus station in David. I have had quite a few people return to my hotel asking to spend an extra night because they missed their flight.

**ProTip:** If you're going by bus, leave Boquete early. You still have to take a taxi out to David's airport.

Seeing someone renting a car at the Panama City airport is heartbreaking. They are eager to enjoy a scenic drive to Boquete, but the problems start when they discover it could be more exciting. Don't fall for the trap. It's not worth the hassle!

Worse yet, it gets complicated and expensive when people want to return the rental car early at David Airport and fly to Panama City. It's ridiculous at the car rental return at the David airport. And you still have to buy a bus or plane ticket to Panama City. Or drive it and learn your lesson. You will get it once you have done it. I know I did.

**ProTip:** How do you avoid arriving here exhausted? Don't spend 6 hours (both coming and going) in a boring car ride on your first visit to Panama. Don't rent a car in Panama City and drive here. Take Copa Airlines the rest of the way. Then, pick up and return your car or 4x4 rental in the David Airport.

I must confess to enjoying the traders and characters who get off and on the buses. It happens frequently on the deluxe double-decker Mercedes Benz buses. They use those to run the Panamerican Highway route between Panama City and David. I like the inflight movies! If you want to take the bus, it is less than $20 between those two city bus stations, both coming and going.

If you take the bus, don't expect to see much. You likely won't see anything outside because the Panamanians close all the bus's drapes to sleep. You can watch the movie on board. You might see evangelical ministers jump on. They are working at saving souls as they roll down the highway. Also, they will stop and let a friendly jewelry salesperson and hot food vendors with icy cold drinks. You can see incredible things on that six-hour run inside the bus, not outside. Remember about the drapes.

I've taken that bus trip many times. I've sat through services quite a few times. Different preachers onboard who run a little church service then pass the hat. Sometimes, a religious film is on to boost inspiration and drama. I have also seen some great action movies in Spanish. They are rarely subtitled. It all depends on which bus line you're taking. Remember to wait for the next *Express* bus. Non-Express buses take forever. There will be a half-hour restaurant and bathroom break during the trip. So don't dilly-dally. Follow the rushing crowd.

**ProTip:** Red Alert! Many times, the bus bathroom could be better. You need to plan. I've often run into a sign that says, you can go #1, not #2 if you know what I mean. Or the bathrooms busted. Out-of-order sign outside.

On the way to Bocas del Toro on the public bus, there is a nice bathroom and meal stop. But if you leave Boquete and want to go to Bocas del Toro by public bus, you must take the bus down to David. That is why public buses take much longer than shuttles between Bocas del Toro and Boquete.

Call my hotel if you want the $35-40 shuttle (including boat taxi) that skips going down the volcano to David. It cuts off a lot of time because it uses the cutoff road via Caldera to Bocas del Toro (the Caribbean side of the country). We are happy to help you get picked up anywhere. We will arrange that even if you're not staying at our hotel.

I am reluctant to give you my last trick, but here is my story. A few years ago, they started buying two-story tall Mercedes-Benz super-buses. Each one costs half a million dollars. They are colder than the back of a butcher shop. So pack a parka. Those Germans can build great air conditioners! The drivers keep it on max, so cold people get hypothermia and get off in the middle of nowhere to recover.

Because of that, several guests haven't shownup on the day of their reservation and canceled with charges but then arrived the next day, wanting to check-in. That's quite a mess if you've already sold their room. So, please don't wear beachwear on that bus! Thank me later.

I like to sit in the front row upstairs because it's all glass. I'm a big guy. I need the extra legroom. You can leave your curtain open, but the front row has no screen to see the movie. But you can watch the country fly by.

Let me warn you: The bus attendant will make you wear a seatbelt in the front row on the second floor. That's in case they slam on the brakes. It is a massive piece of glass up there in front. The guy will check you are wearing them! That goes for all the upper front-row seats.

Chapter 8

# Panama's International Retirement Program

## #1 in the World

Panama makes it hassle-free for U.S. citizens to visit and explore. They may also consider retiring and enjoying a new life in an exotic country. Traveling to Panama is accessible for U.S. citizens. You'll need:

1. You do not need a visa.
2. Bring a valid passport (valid at least six months after arrival).
3. A round-trip ticket (by bus or airline) to leave.

Experience all Panama has to offer. With the Panama International Retirement Program, you can. This Panama program delivers beautiful sights and culture and has a low cost of living. It also has a long list of world-class retirement benefits!

Panama provides more benefits to retirees than any other country in the world. It is one of a kind. Remember, you can apply for permanent residency. Your citizenship must be from a country in the "Friendly Nations Visa" group. These benefits are not exclusive to the foreign-born permanent residents. Panamanian and expatriate retirees get discounts on a lot of stuff in Panama.

## 25% Off Airline Tickets!

The biggest one is a 25% discount on airfare! And not only inside Panama. They include all trips that start here, go anywhere in the world, and return to Panama. You must buy all legs of the ticket together from an authorized seller. *Viajes David* travel agency does that work. They handle all my flight ticketing. They are good at their jobs. I calculate they've saved me over $12,000 over the years.

*Tocumen International Airport* is the regional hub. It links the Caribbean, South, North, and Central America. There are many direct flights to Europe. Panama City, Panama, is a central crossroads of the world. The first time you arrive, you will see it is the skyscraper capital of Latin America. Please notice the famous *Screw-Shaped Tower!* It's one of a kind.

In Panama City, Copa Airlines has its base. And there are twice-daily flights between David and the capital. They sell cheap tickets to Columbia, Ecuador, Bolivia, Paraguay, and Argentina. They are very enticing. Recently, Argentina became a better deal. They recently devalued their currency by half! Those destinations call out to my friends who have wanderlust. Travel sells at a discount when you live in Panama.

Bajo Boquete is the location of the lovely people at *Viajes David* travel agency. *Viajes* means *Trips*. They are across the river from the Gringo Market. They have these insane deals all the time. The deals are for the most amazing destinations. They offer extraordinary trips out of Panama at attractive prices. Everyone says their package deals are fantastic!

There are many discounts for expat residents, including *60-year-old men* and *55-year-old women*. Panamanians get them the same. It's a long list. All it takes is for you to hold an E-Cedula and meet the age rule. Remember, Pensionado Visa holders agree not to work here. That's the deal.

It's simple:

Enjoy incredible discounts on various categories:

- Entertainment: 50% off ball games, concerts, theater, and movies!
- Transportation: 30% off trains, boats, and buses.
- Hotels: 50% off on Mon-Thurs, 30% off on Fri-Sun.
- Restaurant meals: 25% off full meals (no cafés).

- Medical consultations: 20% off.
- Dental and eye exams: 15% off.
- Hospital bills (without insurance): 15% discount.
- Pharmacy prescriptions: 10% off.
- Buying a home? Get 50% off closing costs from the bank.

**Pro-Tip:** The Pricesmart Membership includes a Free Annual Eye Exam and a touchless glaucoma screening test. They did an excellent job on my last set of glasses. Membership costs $35/yr, and the Annual Membership Fee covers two people, reducing the cost to $17.50 per person.

## Panama Loves and Respects Elders

Elders get VIP treatment in Boquete, Panama. Notice the *Jubilado* line at the banks, which has no waiting or much shorter lines. People are kind here. Elders are out and about, walking arm in arm with family members. They don't put them in nursing homes; they tend to keep them at home.

**Pro Tip:** Learn to say "*Descuento de Jubilado, Por Favor.*" That means *Retired Person's Discount, Please.* Offer to show your *ID card* (Panama Cedula) and smile! Say, *"Quieres ver mi Cedula?"* (*Would you like to see my ID?*). It works for full meals only, not at coffee shops.

People notice and speak to elders, and patience is more common here. Boquete may be the best place I have ever seen to raise a child. Panama has a six-day workweek, so Sundays are family-focused. Visit the riverside *Boquete Library Park.* You will see grandparents, parents, kids, and babies together. They lay on blankets in the shade or walk the trails. It is lovely. And they are so friendly!

Expats get extra attention because Panamanians love to practice their English skills. I speak Spanish, which delights them. It's attention-getting when I use local slang. I have observed, met, and gotten to know hundreds of Panamanian families at my hotel.

They come for breakfast and stop in over the holidays. They hang in our hammocks or sit on our terrace or balcony. They try the super oatmeal and enjoy the views. They also want the coffee shop's sandwiches, pastries, and drinks. *Mi casa es Tu casa, (My house is Your home)*.

I soon feel like family. On the first visit comes a young couple. The next visit comes with friends and siblings. Third visit: Mom, Dad, Grandpa, Grandma, Cousins, Kids, and Babies. And last-minute tag-a-longs.

They come begging for extra beds. We have them. The name for a ¾ *Bed* is *Cama Tres Quatro*. They want them in their rooms or a blanket for sleeping in our outdoor hammocks! What a joy they have brought with their gentle nature. Kisses from Grandma and hugs from Pops. There is something special going on here in Boquete, Panama. These are the happy lands.

Chapter 9

# What does the US Government say?

## It is Simple and Easy to Qualify

Don't believe me? Take a quick look at what the U.S. Government says about it on the official website:

https://www.embassyofpanama.org/retire-in-panama

If you're considering emigrating using Panama's Retiree Visa, here's how to make it happen:

1. Seek guidance from an immigration lawyer in Panama.
2. Present evidence of personal income. It should be U.S.$1,000.00/month. Also, show income for dependents. It should be U.S.$250.00/month per dependent.
3. You can change your status after entering on a tourist visa.
4. If applicable, provide certified birth and marriage certificates.
5. Secure an official FBI (or your nation's) police clearance within the valid period.
6. Please authenticate each document. The cost is U.S.$30 per document. You have two options: You can go through Panama's Washington, D.C. Consulate or use the Panama Consulate in the country of your passport.

For more details, see:

https://www.embassyofpanama.org/legalization-of-documents-1

## #1 in the World? - What are My Chances? What do I need?

1. Be at least 18 years old.
2. Engage a Panamanian Attorney to guide you through the application process.
3. Requirements can change unexpectedly. Each case is unique. Seek guidance from a skilled attorney in Panama.
4. Your attorney can help you. They will get the Registration Form from the Immigration Office in Panama City.
5. Submit an original, notarized letter from a private or public entity. The letter should certify your pensioner status and income.
6. You must meet the monthly income rule of U.S.$1000.00. This income must come from a government or private corporation, for example, Social Security, Social Security Disability, or a military pension. For each dependent spouse or minor child, increase the income by U.S.$250.00.
7. Authenticate proof of income with an apostille seal or at the Panamanian Consulate.
8. Get a Health Certificate from a Panamanian Doctor.
9. Authenticate your Certification of No Arrest Data (Police record). F.B.I. background check for U.S. citizens, R.C.M.P. police report with fingerprints for Canadians. Do the authentication through the Panamanian Consulate or Apostille Seal.
10. If you are single, get a bachelorhood certificate or a notarized statement. Have two witnesses present. Get the statement authenticated by the Panamanian Consulate.
11. Prepare four photographs per regulation.
12. Provide a notarized, authenticated photocopy of your passport (including all pages).
13. Prepare a sworn statement about your personal background. Do it in Panama through a lawyer.
14. Keep the original passport available for visa issuance.
15. Be present in Panama during the visa issuance process.

These steps will help ensure a smooth and successful residency application in Panama.

## How about the Wife (or Husband) and Kids?

Are you married and want to include your family? They ask you to prepare the following documents for an efficient procedure.

1. Power of Attorney.
2. Apostille Seal or Panamanian Consulate authenticate the marriage certificate.
3. Get a certificate of "No Arrest Data" for your wife. You must notarize and authenticate them.
4. Birth certificates of children authenticated by the Panamanian Consulate.
5. Photocopy of passport.
6. Four photographs of each dependent.
7. A Panamanian doctor issues a health certificate.
8. A sworn statement about personal background prepared through a lawyer.
9. Responsibility Letter notarized and authenticated by the Panamanian Consulate.

The Panamanian Consulate or Apostille must authenticate all documents issued abroad. You must do this before submitting your paperwork to your attorney in Panama. The Panamanian Consulate can only authenticate U.S.-issued birth and marriage certificates. For documents from other countries, please contact the respective Panamanian Consulate for authentication.

## Panama Pensionado Program Offers Great Incentives:

1. Import tax exempts household goods.
2. The government waives the import tax on new cars every two years, but other taxes apply when importing a vehicle.
3. Enjoy a 25% discount on utility bills.
4. Save 25% on airline tickets and 30% on other transportation.

5. Avail a 15% loan discount in your name.
6. Get a 1% reduction on home mortgages for personal residence.
7. Receive a 20% discount on professional and technical service bills.

## Living in Panama Page

https://pa.usembassy.gov/living-in-panama/

Note: This is a beneficial page on the US Embassy's Website.

Discover:

1. Residence Requirements
2. https://migracion.gob.pa/
3. https://panamadigital.gob.pa/
4. Purchasing Property
5. realestate@panamcham.com
6. *Read the Embassy's Precautions* if you are considering buying property here.
7. Drivers License
8. Disabled Parking Permit
9. Criminal Record Checks

## Panama Consulate Fees

Remember: The fee to authenticate documents is U.S.$30.00 per document. You pay at the Panamanian Consulate in Washington, D.C.

## Panama's Embassy in the United States:

EMBASSY OF PANAMA IN THE UNITED STATES,

2862 MCGILL TERRACE N.W.,

WASHINGTON, D.C. 20008

TEL: +1 (202) 483-1407

EMAIL: INFO@EMBASSYOFPANAMA.ORG

Chapter 10
# Medical Costs

## Go to the Doctor!

I'm getting better. I'm now going to the doctor when I feel bad.
Massive chest pain, boom! I go to the doctor. Jumbo headache that
won't go away? Adios! I'm going to the doctor. It's such a comfort.
Never in my life have I ever been unafraid to go to the doctor. Good
things happen at the doctors here. I can't believe what I am saying. I
have changed that much.

Even working in hospitals, I was a doctor-avoider my whole life.
Sure, they did some nasty things to me dealing with traumas and
heart surgeries but damn! I like the way they doctor here. They treat
you as if you are part of their family or something. Double check call
on you. Pass you around to the other providers like a visiting guest
from the royal families of Europe. I've got a new normal here.

So my new normal is: I don't feel well, so I go to the doctor and soon
get better. Here is a helpful link to a list, in English, for healthcare in
Chiriqui Province:

https://chiriqui.life/topic/1743-health-care-resources-for-the-
chiriqui-province/.

## Emergency Room in Boquete

I already told you about the Public Health Clinic in Boquete
charging only $.50 for stitches. Now, I will tell you a story about
some friends, then a couple about me. I have a Canadian "snowbird"
buddy (six months here/then six there). He is a pretty tough guy.
Canada seems to build men and women that way. We have become
friends.

His mama watched him from home as he played hockey on the street
in front of his house. Like me, he enjoyed ice fishing out of semi-

permanent housing on three feet of ice with bored holes. He is so tough; he went out and helped me batten the hatches down at the hotel in a hurricane-force storm. That's why I gave him his nickname, "Mountain Man."

Even electric bikes are good for your health. Mountain Man rents them from the spot next to our Brew Pub, one block from my hotel. He'd been renting one for the five to six months here. During last year's visit, he turned too tight on loose gravel near *Mike's Global Grill* and fell severely the day before his departure, landing head first, right on his eye!

What they say about head wounds is true. They are gushers. So, someone hauled him to the public health emergency ward. He protested loudly and bled emphatically.

I know many staff members, nurses, medical doctors, and directors at that location. They are familiar with me as well. Before, the clinic received a fresh coat of paint from the Rotary Club during my presidency. The members also constructed new public bathrooms and a biomedical/hazardous waste lockup. The day he fell, my buddy needed a friend to assist with translation and help sort him out.

They got him to me with his phone so the Attending Physician could speak with me. This public health medical doctor confirmed I knew him. I advised him that screaming was not his typical nature. "Please come now! He is not being violent at all, only loud!" He'd had a severe blow to the head. He was not his usual, quiet Canadian self.

I could hear him from the back as I entered. I saw his head wound had painted him red from head to toe. No doubt. He had a concussion. They feared he had suffered an orbital fracture of his eye as well.

He was a bit confused because of the trauma. He refused the free ambulance trip to The Regional David Hospital for a scan and x-rays. I called our friend who rents the E-bikes, and he came down and took him to the hospital himself.

After stitching him up, they asked us to pass by the cashier to pay his bill before departing. In the commotion, we misheard the price. I figured for all that they had done, it had to be at least $50, not $.50. My buddy told me he didn't have enough cash to cover his prescriptions plus the bill.

I told him not to worry and that I would pay for it. So, in the confusion, I gave the cashier $50 in cash, and the lady laughed and said, "No! Fifty cents! Only two quarters. That's all!" You are going to love Panama!

He kept singing at the ambulance guy, "I don't need an ambulance!" The ambulance driver joined those sweet nurses, and they all said, in chorus, "No, Mister! Ambulance Free!" But like a lousy cow-dog, he refused to load up.

He's a big man and not his usual self. He yelled, "NO! No Ambulance! I'm not going!" He had it fixed in his head, but jumping in with the electric bike guy was a different deal! The nice electric bike guy took him at no charge, paid for all the rest, fed him, collected the e-bike, and brought him home.

The *Hospital Centro Medico Mae Lewis* got him x-rayed and scanned. There was no subdural hematoma on his brain or orbital fracture by the eye. He flew home the next day. Tuff guy! He had some floaters in his vision, but less now.

I am overwhelmed by his transformation. Last month, I saw him laughing while walking downtown with friends. He lost a bunch of weight, got fit, and now has gone full *Pickleball!* It is excellent for your health. That sport is like tennis, using a unique racket and ball. It is the latest craze to hit our valley. The number of folks playing it here has exploded. New courts are under construction in Bajo Boquete.

They say pickleball is the fastest-growing sport in the world. It sure grew fast here. I heard two individuals are giving free lessons! We have a very active, retired, expat crowd in Boquete. They are outgoing. They often do meals or coffee together, creating connections. Yes, having friends is good for your health.

# Medical Emergency Services

I've had a few breathing crises. Boquete's Public Health Emergency Department managed the most recent one. They had to give me two rounds of nebulizer treatments followed by I.V. steroids to line it out.

Emergency Services is next door to the Romero grocery store. It is the green building on the corner. My main pre-heart surgery symptom of *S.O.B.*, or Shortness of Breath, can still haunt me. I'm susceptible to bleach, ammonia, and cleaning supplies. They fill my lungs with fluid. It's like I'm suffocating.

Years back, I was in the middle of a crisis. I visited my local Private Doctor, *Dr. Gonzalez*. He sent me straight away to David to see *Dr. Rodriguez*. He was first a *Cardiologist* but returned to school because he loved *Pulmonology*. His old office was inside the front door of *Chiriqui Hospital*, but he has since moved to his new location outside the hospital.

On my last visit, I was in bad shape. Dr. Rodriguez sent me downstairs for X-rays. He discovered my heart was now standard size! That made my day. He also did a full work-up on me with spirometry and dispensed a big bag of free medication. That visit only cost me $97! Was the bill a misprint? $97? They must be missing a zero. Can it be that cheap here? It explains why so many expats are *self-insured.*

I was doing that for a while. For private care, I have to pay out of pocket. I do that if I'm too sick to wait in line. Plus, I use the Public Clinic as primary care. Recently, I got back under Panama's Social Security health insurance.

It covers me because I am an employee of my hotel's corporation. I don't wait for Public or Social Security to do an in-system referral to see medical specialists. I almost always pay out of pocket.

I hold a *work permit*. Last year, I returned to my hotel's payroll with an employment contract. That gets me into the worker's *Social Security* healthcare system. The same is true for all contracted workers and their families here.

I was able to do that because I hold a work permit. That was possible because I moved to the country through the *Friendly Nation Investor Visa Program.* Let's be clear. You can't do this if you move here on the retiree visa program.

Let me tell you about a chat I had with Dr. Gonzalez at the beginning of the COVID-19 pandemic. I asked him if I should get private insurance because of my health situation. His answer shocked me.

"Tim, I don't have private insurance either. You don't need to spend money on that. I don't. You are a permanent resident here. You can access the Public Healthcare System like Panamanians."

He got on his soapbox. "That's one of the secret benefits of living here that most expats don't understand. If you have a burst Appendix and go to a Public or Private Hospital, you go to surgery equally fast. And the same doctor will probably operate on you!" How about that?

# Chapter 11
# High Tech Dentists

I call my buddy from Hawaii "Maui John." He is a retired guy who stayed in my hotel a few years ago. He loves to scuba dive in all the best places around the world. He knew I was a Dentist/Prosthetic Surgeon and called me. He wondered if I could recommend a Dentist here who could handle a big case like he needed. He'd gotten a quote from a dentist in Hawaii for about $30,000, plus a quote for cosmetic veneers for an extra $7,500.

I often refer people to my ex-sister-in-law, the famous *Dr. Luz Barria-Cruz*, (+507-6982-2902). She speaks English and is my General Dentist and is located next to Al Punto restaurant. She is great and well known for being gentle. She lives and works here in Bajo Boquete.

I told John to send me his treatment plan. It was an extremely challenging case. Before my advanced training, I usually sent these complex cases to a Prosthodontist/Implant Surgeon specialist. He needed quite a few surgeries. The plan included bone grafts and skin grafts. It also involved complex implant-supported bridgework and many root canal treatments. That's stuff I used to do, prosthodontist-level work.

So, I sent him to the Clinica Dental Especializada Halfen in David, (+507-6071-7500). *The Halfen Specialized Clinic* is an Implant and Oral Rehabilitation Center. The father and son have helped me many times. The son attended Mexico's U.A.G. Dental School (Universidad Autónoma de Guadalajara). That was before his specialty training—small world. Years ago, the Dean of my Dental School sent me down to Mexico. He sent me to become U.A.G.'s first summer exchange student from my school, O.U.C.O.D. - Oklahoma University College of Dentistry.
https://clinicahalphen.com.pa/

The young Dr. Frank Halfin and his dad did their first CAD/CAM (computer-generated) all-ceramic crowns on me. These crowns are beautiful, strong, precise, and resist the growth of dental plaque, which helps if you have gum disease.

That was when they first got the technology I used back in Montana. They wanted my input. They have the new 3D Panoramic X-ray machine and do high-tech stuff like I did for years. Maui John was pleased with their work. The final cost was about half of the Hawaii quote, so he still had money set aside and elected for full Veneers! He looks great!

Here's one more good dental story. I've got a friend named *Dr. Juan Carlos Ortiz*. He runs a group practice called Odonto Advance, Odontología de Precisión (Precision Dentistry). He's an Endodontist and speaks English. They are the root canal guys. His specialty Dental clinic, *https://www.odontoadvance.com/*(+507-6130-4820), is across the street from Chiriqui Hospital in David.

His associate did some beautiful bonding on my front tooth and is soon replacing a large restoration this week. Dr. Ortiz is the president and founder of the Microscope Dentistry Association. Last year, he finished and published the textbook on this new dental specialty.

We've gotten well acquainted over the years. I've got what you could call *Cowboy Teeth*. Many cracks are present in places that should never crack. There is random pain that's hard to figure out where it's coming from, even with the microscope he uses.

I'd had a rough landing in a flood in David. I'd almost crashed my 4x4 in a cement ditch and bounced my head off the window. He took the standard X-rays, but they didn't show where my pain was coming from. He insisted that I go across the street for a CAT- scan. I tried to refuse, but hell, it was only $89! I walked the DVD-R, where they recorded it, back across the street. He put it in his fancy computer to look at it together.

**Pro Tip:** You must buy and bring a DVD-R for Medical X-rays and Scans. You will be given your DVD-R with a copy of the images they created. Later, you will get your report from the Radiologist.

As he spun my skull around in 3D, we both spotted the problem. We both jumped like spooked jackrabbits. I had what dentists eloquently nick-named *The Heart Stopper Abscess*. I had a hole in the tongue side of my lower jaw. It was the size of a 45-caliber slug.

That means it's been there a while. And it explains why I've been so sick these last few years. Lol! He does have a hole in his head! Good grief! The tooth had hidden the drain hole on the x-ray. The abscess was draining inside my body.

We all have potential spaces, like how chicken comes apart in chunks. That hole lined up with the connected spaces that pass by the tongue, down the neck, into the sack around the heart. Gentle Jesus! We looked at each other in shock and understanding.

I love that guy! He saved my life. He orchestrated the fancy surgery to save the front half of that molar and get it crowned. He brings many advanced dental practitioners into his clinic. A lovely lady periodontist performed my hemi-section surgery in his office. That means she split the molar and extracted the back half. Young Dr. Frank Halfen crowned the front.

It's about time to get a follow-up scan. I'm still having some odd pain on that side. But you know, cowboys. We'll see how it turns out. But that shows you how good dental care is in Panama.

Chapter 12

# Safe and Secure Community

## Extra Police Force = The Tourist Police

A few years ago, a group of Policemen I knew invited me to drink soda pop and eat little sandwiches. They were trying to start a new program. I give all the Policemen who serve in Boquete free coffee. They can get it anytime at my Café Central, the coffee shop at Hotel Central Boquete. To say I know a lot of cops here is an understatement.

These folks make little money. Many spend weeks away from their families while risking their lives protecting us. They were nice enough to explain what they were doing. A team of the local cops I knew had taken *Community Policing* training. Part of their mission was reaching out to people like me. They wanted my support.

They extended an invitation to hotel and hostel owners and managers. They desired to collaborate with them. As a result, we established *Hoteles Vigilantes Boquete* (*Vigilant Boquete Hotels*). That is a WhatsApp group. The qualified members are all hotel businesses and the Police. With this tool, we can seek help or identify troublemakers before situations escalate. The banner states, *"¡Cuidado, Estamos Mirando!" (Careful, We're Watching!)*.

We soon voted in officers and had many more meetings. Right away, it got traction. We use that closed/private group to inform others about various problems. As owners, managers, and employees of hotels and hostels, we networked. We have come to rely on each other and the local police force. They watch that group. The reaction is fast, fair-minded, and decisive. I never thought it would become so helpful.

We have National Police, Transit Police, Local Police, Large-Disturbance Brigades, and Border Police. Don't freak out when you see the transit cops. Many people do when they get here. They see two scary officers with machine guns on a big motorcycle. The officers are wearing full combat gear.

Because Boquete is a tourist area, we also have teams working night and day as *Tourist Police*. Walking at night, they spook me when they call out my name from the shadows.

They also have undercover cops. I was out for a stroll by myself, late at night, in a crowded festival downtown. Up comes a beautiful young woman walking along beside me. She strikes up what would look like a normal conversation to most people. As you remember from my earlier story, I worked for the government in risky locations. Places they couldn't get regular dentists to go or stay. So, I'm hyper-vigilant. And I'm no dummy. I confronted her. "You're a cop, right?"

"Why would you say that?" I told her, "You're hotter than a three-dollar pistol, and you're not a prostitute." She looked shocked and confessed that she was undercover. She asked, "How did you know?" I filled her in on my past work history and explained. "Your questions are all wrong. You moved too fast. You started with, 'Where am I from'. Then you moved straight to, 'Do I feel safe here?' Then you confirmed you were an undercover cop. You did this by saying, 'Have I seen or experienced anything illegal.'" She stopped and stared at me with a blank face.

Then I said, " And I'm pretty sure that's a pistol you're packing under your pretty skirt! Isn't it?" She looked shocked, guilty as charged. Instantly, she turned on her cop persona. She asked if I knew about or had seen any crimes. They had gotten reports of a gang of pickpockets. I told her it was great she was there; no, I had not.

Take action. Increase your security when you move here. Many parts of the valley have formed *Vecinos Vigilante* or *Vigilant Neighbors*. They are our Neighborhood Watch groups. Look for their signs when you move here. Either join up or get one started. It makes a difference.

# The Police Stop on the Way into Town

Another reason Boquete is safe is our *Police Checkpoint,* or *Retén de Policia,* south of town on the main road to David. Smile as you come to it. You are on *candid camera.* They have face and car tag recognition cameras there and around town. Panama is the wrong country to be a wanted criminal. That checkpoint is the clinching point for getting in and out of here. Boquete is up at the end of the road with four paved loops that access the Boquete valley. On satellite views or road maps, it looks like a four-leafed clover.

**Pro Tip:** Don't leave home without your Panamanian ID or Passport. There are Police Checkpoints all over Panama, and random document checks can happen. Tourists on day trips have been stopped and sent to get them.

Be careful in the rain or fog; our police checkpoint can sneak up on you and surprise you. That happened to me once. I scared the, you know what, out of myself. The police stop is *north* of the enormous *Faro (Lighthouse),* between David and Boquete. It and the *Los Molinos (The Mills)* gated community entry are on your left or west side. You'll see those first before the cop-stop.

I was creeping along, heading back to Boquete in a pea-soup fog. Out of nowhere, the Police Checkpoint appeared! I almost ran right into it! What a close call! When tired, exercise caution, particularly in conditions of limited visibility.

Fog, rain, and nighttime conditions can lead to disaster. Pull off the road if you must stop! You could get hit from behind. Use extra caution at night. Slow down to avoid deep water. Poorly lit vehicles may pose a hazard. We have whiteouts from blinding fog or rain. People in dark clothes strolling on the side of the road add to the risks.

## Police Stop - Check Point

What are the best practices at the police stop? As you pull up, open your front windows, put your two hands on the wheel, turn on the interior light, if at night, and smile. Thank them for their service.

Keep your documents organized. Carry your passport if you still need to get your Panamanian Documents. Ask them how they are. Do it in English; they will usually wave you right through, though only sometimes. That's what I call, *show-em your gringo face.*

They serve out of a concrete-reinforced little shack in the middle of the road. Keep your proof of insurance and driver's license close. If you are on a tourist visa, your U.S. license lets you drive for three months. You have a problem if they catch you after that. Then your insurance isn't valid, and you have two issues. Don't add a third! Those two little buildings on the right of the checkpoint are a holding jail cell and a mini judge's office.

We have whiteouts from blinding fog, with and without rain. Black horses, cows, dogs, and people wearing dark clothes can be on the road. And they're often not walking against traffic but with it. Pedestrians walking on the wrong side of the road are seen frequently at night. We need more sidewalks.

Slow down to avoid hydroplaning in deep water. There is a curve at the bridge north of the *Federal Mall.* It collects water and causes many accidents. That mall is between us and David. You must take it on your way into the City of David. It's the most extensive and newest shopping mall in the country.

Keep your driver's license, proof of insurance, and certified inspection document close when driving. Cops on motorcycles make random stops at the craziest locations. Be prepared. They are not messing around. They set up police stops at odd places. Once, my car got towed, and I got fined. My passport stamp was too old. I had gone over the three-month grace period by four days.

Back then, I did not have a Panamanian driver's license. I had my passport, a valid Montana (U.S.A.) driver's license, and proof of insurance coverage. You can drive legally here for only three months. After that, your insurance is no good. So that was two strikes against me. I should have checked my passport. And I should've asked someone with a license to drive for me. Get your Panama driver's License ASAP. Towing, Fine, and taxis cost me almost $400!

**Pro Tip:** I recently learned that the three-month grace period is lost after you get your permanent visa!

I forgot to dim my lights twice when pulling up to the police stop. It is irritating and suspicious. They will think you've been drinking. You will get a mini-lecture while they check you out. Dim your headlights and smile! There is a face-scanning security camera. And it reads your car's license plate number. We have a few cameras in our valley. A well-dressed security team of police officers monitors the system. They and the system's control office are in the Police building.

## Bad Hideout For Criminals

My college roommate was from Panama. When I was a teenager, he told me something funny: "You've got to be an idiot to be a crook in my country." The country is long and skinny. There's only one road through it. There's nowhere to get away! We have a small population. Everybody knows everybody. And they love to talk!"

## Criminals Get Caught

Don't come here if you are running from the law! Lol! They have security camera systems throughout the nation. Panama could be a better place to hide out. Ten years ago, there was an *Interpol* team that collected dozens of pedophiles in the Highlands! They had new technology. They extracted videos from collected computers. Then, they retrieved the suspects' faces from reflections, like shiny spoons on the table. We don't need your kind around here!

Get the rest of the story. I wonder why people tell me all the secrets of what's happening here. They were hiding in our hills. Those Interpol guys were brilliant. They went all over. The Interpol agents met and flirted with little old ladies in the back of Beyond. The ladies sell lunch, snacks, and cold soda pop from their homes. They see everything going on!

They first figured out what section of the country they were living in. They would show them a book full of pictures and explain. "Ma'am, they are afraid of going into town. They pay people to buy and deliver their groceries and supplies. They may stop at your place. Don't show any emotion if you recognize one. There are bad people on these pages. Call us, and we will come right away!"

**Pro-tip:** Try this experiment. Make sure you present yourself in the best way possible. Put your best foot forward. For example, you enter a business in the morning. There are lots of workers and waiting customers. Joyfully announce yourself. That's super Panamanian! Do it with a loud, friendly *"Buenos Dias"!* It's marvelous when they all look up, stop what they're doing, then smile and wish you a *Good Morning*.

## Caring Community and Gated Community

The safest place is next to a big, raucous Panamanian family in town. Take note. I sell great earplugs at my hotel. You are going to need them to sleep during the holidays. Trust me, it's never a dull moment. Those periodically noisy neighbors? They've got your back! We have many gated communities here with security at the entry. But we also have a very caring community of Panamanians, Indigenous, and foreigners. We all watch out for each other. I remember the many incredible kindnesses I saw during the pandemic. It brings tears to my eyes.

**ProTip:** When you move into town, make friends with your neighbors. I recommend offering them baked chili beans, cornbread, honey, and butter. That's a cheap, neighborly gift. The Panamanians will love it. Southern-style cornbread is a novelty here.

When you deliver it, offer to teach their kids and grandkids English! Offer a trade-off for Spanish Lessons. It will pay untold dividends in your safety and happiness. Say, *¡Bueno-Bueno!* in the morning. That means *Good!* Look at the people. The locals love that! Smile! It will increase your face value.

Yes, we have locals who drive Ferraris! Many wealthy foreigners live in *McMansions,* far from their neighbors. Expensive vehicles, flashy rings, watches, or jewelry can make you a target. It is prudent to *dress down* here. Be aware of your surroundings and the image you project in public.

Chapter 13
# Local & National Parks

## Boquete Riverside Library Park

You will love this park. It's so incredible! And it is FREE! It is four blocks from *Parque Central* (*Central Park*) in Bajo Boquete. It can be a bit tricky to find. Go to the *Biblioteca* (*Library*) on *Avenida Central* (*Central Avenue*). Then, head east toward our *Rio Caldera* (*Caldera River*). The river is on the east side of town at the base of the mountains. Central Avenue is the road you came in on from David.

You can park on the side of the road in those parking spots beside the park. Don't hit the tree branches. After turning left at the green gated park entry, you will see them there. Then go north (the only way you can go; the road turns left ). The park's parking lot entrance is next to a new restaurant being built now. Immediately turn *right* to get inside. Also, a new pedestrian gate is next to one of my favorite restaurants, *Malú*.

On Sundays, there might be a total traffic jam. We can get bumper-to-bumper gridlock inside that parking lot. Watch out for that. The park opens at 6 AM and closes at 5:30 PM. The gate for the parking lot has a grace period that ends at 6 PM. The staff locks the other entries at 5:30 PM. You must walk north to the parking lot if you parked under the trees I wrote about. Then, exit the main gate and walk the street back south to your car.

The theme is nature, like Central Park in New York City. The land buy and development came through the Peterson Family's Foundation. The father, Price Peterson, is my friend. The Library Foundation of Boquete, https://www.biblioboquete.com/, runs it. Their Foundation also helped build the Boquete Library. It was Panama's first *lending* library. Lol! They told Price, "You want to send kids home with books? They won't bring them back! You can't do that here." That's not the vision he had for our new library.

It is a beautiful place. It's all glass and three stories tall. It holds many fine collections and art and a sizable meeting room on the third floor. It has a great staff, led by *Elsa*, its talented director. On the southwest side of the second floor, they have a sizable collection of books written in English. They frequently have meetings, live music, exhibitions, and talks there.

**Pro Tip:** Get your free library card by showing a utility bill or rental contract.

I am good friends with everyone involved in the new park. A diverse coalition has moved this project forward. There is an *arborist* or *tree specialist*. I met her when she worked with a large crowd that came to plant new native trees to aid in reforesting Panama. We in Rotary have planted trees since the start of the park. Now, some are as high as an elephant's eye.

I am so blessed to have all these park people and wildlife in my life. Later, more than 20 turtles, baby ducks, and comical fresh-born armadillos joined. Dancing plover birds also arrived. Diving ducks, giant white cranes, red tilapia, and koi fish followed. I once saw millions of baby frogs erupt in the area of the new ponds.

This week, I posted a lucky video on my YouTube Channel, *Panama-Loco*. I'd been observing a nested pair of eagles across the river. I recorded a dramatic dive and catch of a large fish in the upper pond. That eagle struggled to fly away with that thrashing fish in its sharp talons.

And now, whole families are surfing blankets in the shade. Elders sit on benches. Kids kick a soccer ball. Barefoot walkers *ground* themselves. Babies crawl over fine sod-planted grass. This pond-filled riverside park is the perfect place. Stretch your legs, people-watch, or take a siesta under a shade tree.

But my greatest joy is watching how much Price Peterson enjoys being there. I watch him, delighted, chatting up the visiting children and families. Our mayor and his wife love this Library Park. They're my friends. Those two have fallen head over heels for it, too.

I'll never forget when I caught the mayor merrily digging a huge hole to plant a new tree. Dirt covered him from head to toe! It's funny how, one day, he's doing manual labor. The following month, he introduced me to a group of mayors and the ambassador from El Salvador. Like I'm some V.I.P. around here. But let me be clear: I'm not!

I can't wait to see what's going to happen next. Price Peterson wants to build a place for music performances. He wants to keep the park all rustic. His goal is to leave it natural and undeveloped. But imagine a sundown concert with a backdrop of Volcano Baru! He showed me where an Architect designed a footbridge across the Caldera to the area he had in mind.

The smaller river that comes from Valle Escondido has a new arch bridge. It connects the northern pair of the three sections of the park. The middle area is still quite rustic, with no paved trails. They have started the southern/third section. It goes down to the *Puente Zarzo* (*Wattle Bridge*) footbridge. They have cleared off the Caldera River stone levee down there. It is still a work in progress. They are building a new bridge for pedestrians and cars to replace the Zarzo.

Price Peterson always says, "Maybe a hundred years!" when people ask him for a completion date. "The ones to come will add their touch to what we have started here."

## Many Hiking Trails and Hiking Groups!

An ever-expanding stretch of night-lit, asphalt-paved trail passes under the new Boquete bridge. This new attraction is the picturesque *Panamonte Bridge* over the *Caldera River*, built with protected pedestrian walkways. This week, I met the engineer and his team, who are in the middle of expanding it down to the Flower Fair area 200 meters and up to the north another 600 meters! It has many benches where you can enjoy the sun setting over Volcano Baru while you are at the riverside.

I'm a member of a Facebook group called "Take a Hike Boquete" that *Roger Imerman* is leading. He does great. The "Lazy Person's Hiking Club" Facebook group resembles my speed.

I need to catch up with all the hiking groups! I saw a large gang of expats with daypacks and walking sticks meeting outside *Multibank a month ago*. Search on Facebook for the groups with the word "Boquete" in them. Join up and start asking around. There's a group of people much older than I am that I need help to keep up with. I know there's a bunch of ladies that hike, too. But I keep seeing different groups out in the middle of nowhere. People get permission to hike trails on private land, which is nice.

Our best, pay-to-use trails are north of town, next to *Amistad International Peace Park. Amistad* means *Friendship*. It's on the north side of Boquete and is an international park. It extends much farther into Costa Rica. It is an enormous tropical wilderness. That's one of our two neighboring National Parks. It is the largest and contains the challenging *Quetzal Trail*. It passes along the Continental Divide North of the volcano.

The *Pipeline Trail* (*Sendero Acueducto*) is flat. It's an easy to medium-difficulty trail, costing less than $10 per person. It conceals the most enormous tree I've ever seen outside of the redwoods in California. Many miss this big grandpa tree. It is on the left, almost hidden. Look for a hole in the jungle near the big waterfall at the end of the tail. It is on the left side while going in.

Hike in silence. This hiking trail has many *Resplendent Quetzals* living there. It is the most beautiful bird in the world. Their tails can reach 3 feet long! Arrive early. There is an open area in the jungle near the entry. That is where you might see a rare sighting of them on the ground. They gather after the first light of the day. They are scarce and beautiful. This boxed canyon has one of the most healthy populations.

Look for the giant spring on the right side of the trail. That's where Boquete gets its water. Notice the moss-covered aqueduct. It's a huge pipe. You must take it. You will be hiking next to it most of the way. Don't be a goofball, and try walking on it. It's slippery as snot. That's how people break their arms. Attorneys have told me that the legal term for this is an *attractive hazard.*

# Volcan Baru National Park

The other Park is *Volcano Barú National Park*, on the west side of town. Many people would like to summit this highest spot in the country. They come from the far side (at Cerro Punta Ranger Station) and then descend to us, or they go up and down from our side's Ranger station.

National Parks surround us on two sides, north and west! To the east are the enormous Indigenous reserve lands called the *Comarca Ngäbe-Buglé*, which the government of Panama created in 1997.


# The Pipeline Trail

The *Sendero Aquiducto (Pipeline Trail)* is in and out, going to the end of a jungled-up box canyon. It follows the town's water supply pipe and has many interesting bridges. It is an excellent trail for young children; it is easy for them.

It has many Blue Morpho butterflies. They are the world's most beautiful butterflies. Keep your eyes peeled. Pay attention. You, too, will start to see them and their flash-like glowing blue metal wings. Once you've seen one, you'll start noticing them all over the valley.

They like squished guava fruit. They feed on the pink, fragrant interiors under those trees. They are iridescent blue while flying. On the ground, they close their wings and disappear with leaf-like camouflage. We once saw a dozen in the trees west of the library park's new arched bridge! You'll know the spot when you see guava fruit squished on the trail.

One day, I was chatting with a friendly retired luxury yacht captain at the back of my hotel. He is now a farmer. He grows pineapples and plantains on a small island he owns in the Bocas del Toro Province near *Red Frog Marina*. Out of nowhere, an *Albino* Blue Morpho butterfly danced around our heads. That pure white butterfly stayed with us for about a minute. Stunned, we sat silent for a while. "Damn showy place you got here, Timmy!" I said in near disbelief,

"So you saw it too? A white morpho? I didn't have a vision?" "Yeah, I saw it too!" "Wow!"

## Lost Waterfalls Trail

If you take a right turn, you will soon run into the *Three Lost Waterfalls* or *Las Tres Cascadas Perdidas*. Otherwise, you will go straight into the *Pipeline Trail*. It costs $10, has three magnificent waterfalls, and much of it is as steep as stairs! It's one of our most demanding trails. Passing the second waterfall can get slippery, and many people slip, slide, and get coated with mud. It is a riskier hike when wet, and unfortunately, some people break arms and legs, so be careful. And use the ropes and switchbacks. That is safer.

Because of this muddy trail, I put in a wash station for muddy boots and tennis shoes at my hotel. I included a rack and clothesline to dry out people's gear. People return to the hotel with taxi man's newspapers glued to one side. They do that to protect the upholstery of their cab. One side was wholly mud-covered, head to toe, and I asked, "So how were the three lost waterfalls trail? Did you reach the third waterfall or slide backward before it?" Lol!

## The Quetzal Trail

There is no charge for the challenging Quetzal Trail. It is in the Amistad National Park. It begins at the end of the road. Go past the Lost Waterfalls Trail, about one steep paved mile to the Ranger Station. It will often be pretty chilly up that high. This long trail follows the Continental Divide in the *Cordillera de Talamanca (Talamanca Mountain Range)*.

This challenging trail passes the volcano's north side to a small farming village near Costa Rica called Cerro Punto. Many hikers start there as it is a higher elevation than our end, and thus, it is easier going downhill. You can find a service to bring your luggage or big pack to our side. Many have done that for a stay in my hotel.

# Amistad International Peace Park

A large Park Ranger station at our trail's end is an entry to Amistad Peace Park. The whole trail is inside this huge National Park, its lands extending far into Costa Rica. You will need to sign in and leave your passport number. You should have a licensed guide when you hike to the Volcan Barú National Park summit. It is not only wise; it's the law.

If you drive south from my hotel, you will find the signs for Volcan Baru National Park. Take your first right, then the second right. This road splits in two immediately. Take the right fork. Notice the new huge sign with tiny lettering. Stop. Take a picture and read it on the way up.

I suggest *an easy-going town trail to my super-fans*. In Bajo Boquete, there are two big bridges over the Caldera River. One is in north Bajo Boquete, close to my hotel. It is the Panamonte Bridge. It is next to the famous Panamonte Hotel, founded in 1904. John Wayne stayed and drank in the bar in the back. It still has two cozy fireplaces. So did many of the first movie stars and various historical figures. It is our longest-serving hotel.

**Pro-tip:** *Boquete* means *Gap or Hole* in English. We are in a notch of Volcano Baru. Coming from the lower lands of David, the names confuse us. When you enter the Boquete area, you first pass *Alto* or *High(Upper)* Boquete. Then you arrive at *Bajo* or *Low(Lower)* Boquete. Going up the Volcano, you climb in altitude. They should be named opposite. Both have deep protected valleys. However, the second neighborhood is lower and is called Bajo Boquete.

The other bridge is in south Bajo Boquete (two blocks east of Central Park). Both connect the east and west sides of the Rio Caldera. Using those two bridges, I often walk with my super-fans in a big circle. On this self-guided hike, you will catch great views and incredible photos from both sides of the river.

# Stay Alive

Be sure to walk on the side of the street that goes against traffic, especially if there's no sidewalk. Pedestrians have no functional rights here. They often don't stop for folks in crosswalks. Always look back at oncoming traffic, even on a sidewalk! Please be careful. Watch for trip hazards! This valley has many. And use extra caution at night. Walk with a flashlight to avoid falls. Clip one of the small, powerful ones to your keys to keep it handy.

Bring extra food, water, rain gear, and warm clothes when hiking our mountain trails. Always tell someone when you'll be back and when you want them to call the police if you don't return! I'm not kidding! It makes it easy for us to send out search and rescue teams to find you if you get lost.

Please understand what I'm about to tell you. We are next to the most dangerous tropical wilderness in the world, 3 1/2 miles from my hotel and on the other side of the continental divide. I've been there, joining the military, police, guides, and firefighters. We searched for and rescued two hotel guests who stayed with us about five years ago. Seeing is believing.

This wilderness is almost impenetrable and deadly treacherous. There are narrow trails at the bottom of deep clefts with solid growth above you. You can touch the walls on both sides as you go. Almost dark on a sunny day. In the dry season, you may traverse knee-deep mud. It can flush you out like a high-pressure toilet in the wet season.

The first of two trails that enter this hazardous wilderness is *El Sendero Pianista*. Or the Pianist Trail. That's the trail where the two young Dutch ladies disappeared. Kris Kremers and Lisanne Froon got lost April 1, 2014. Questions still linger about the circumstances surrounding their disappearance. Following an extensive search on June 19, 2014, they discovered their remains.

# The Snake Trail

The other is the *Sendero Culebra,* or Snake Trail, where we searched for and rescued my two lost hotel guests. They survived by hiding in an unoccupied mountain lion cave! Get a licensed guide! You won't regret it. Plus, they'll teach and show you things you would never notice. Do you feel like that's too much money? Go in a group and share the cost.

> **Pro tip:** The last trail you will enjoy learning about differs from a walking trail. It's a car drive. It is the "lucky-four-leaf clover" motoring self-guided tour of Boquete Valley. Nonstop, it takes a few hours, but it is a one—or two-day drive if you stop for pictures or coffee often.

Pull up a town map and notice the four asphalt-paved loops attached to downtown Bajo Boquete. I named my hotel Hotel Central Boquete because these four paved loop roads end in the center. I recommend doing them counterclockwise. You will only go up super steep sections. It's better to go down them. Don't ride your brakes—pump them. Don't get in a rush. Take breaks to let your transmission and brakes cool off.

## World Famous Birding

Boquete is a *Top 10 Birding Destination in the World.* We have a handful of world-class professional birding guides here. They have telescopes where you can hook up your cell phone to video and take pictures of rare sightings. My hotel guests bring home the most outstanding images and videos! They prove witness to rare dwarf owls dining on lizards!

These adventurous birding guides know where nesting sites are. They go off-trail and are well-trained and licensed. Go online and search for birding here. Notice the long lists of rare birds that live here year-round and those that migrate throughout the year.

We attract the world's most outstanding competitive birders and bird researchers. I have hosted guests from www.birding.com, the Smithsonian Institute, and National Geographic. Additionally, I've hosted many Ph.D.s and Ph.D. candidates. I've also hosted top birding book authors and wealthy retirees who travel the world. They spend all their time birding.

True story: There was an epic birding showdown between two pairs of Swedish cousins. They were the sons of champions from neighboring villages. It was a nail-biting match, reminiscent of their fathers' legendary duel years ago! I met them in the early morning. They were wearing very high-tech, crazy outfits with built-in electronics. They laughed when I asked if they were snipers on a SWAT team.

The world's most famous raptor guy came from Belgium. He said he kept the best for last. He was working hard to finish his book's last chapter on Panama. But he needed photos. That bird guy passed out 50-dollar bills to taxi men to search for rare raptors he could bag. He carried the most damaged-looking long barrel camera I'd ever seen. But what great pics he brought back from trips with those speedy cab drivers!

They paved the street circling the hotel's east side. A short loop starts at my hotel's back terrace. It is fantastic for birding. You may spot woodpeckers, bluebirds, turkeys, parrots, songbirds, and hawks. I have taken these birding people on this 20-minute walk. They go nuts with their binoculars, spotting birds and logging in their journals. They make first-time sightings, much to their delight.

I have seen many weird birds at my hotel passing through Central America. We now have a couple of families of the rare Red-Legged Honeycreeper. They are not hummingbirds but feed at the hotel's hummingbird feeder. They have fire-engine red legs.

The male is black with shiny blue chrome and a light blue cap, and the female is yellow with green chrome. Their only thing in common is their red legs. Birding people think they are a big deal.

We also have swarms of bright baby hummingbirds. Dozens all balled up bounce through the breakfast eaters on the terrace. They are very showy with a solid metallic glow. When young, they can not twist their feathers to camouflage themselves. Only adults can do that. The hummingbird feeder draws them there. I planted bougainvillea flowers along our drive-through coffee. They like those as well. It is the only drive-through coffee in the country.

So get the *best coffee in a cup* and go birding! Lol! Park in the back, come onto the terrace, lay in one of our hammocks, and wait for the gray *Tropical Mockingbirds*. They come to feast on our yard's bugs and worms. Yes, go birding from a hammock at *the home of the latte*. Do it while holding our *famous BLT sandwich*. What a country! You can't make this stuff up!

## Rainbow Ridge

Also, we have many red-neck and black-necked buzzards everywhere. The steep face of Rainbow Ridge, towering above the hotel, attracts them. A protected nesting site is below the town's big lighted cross at the south end. A considerable flock (hundreds!) visits hatchlings one by one.

They are super social. These swarms gather and roost or ride the updraft, patiently waiting their turn. They cover all the trees and the fence and hang in the air, soaring as a group. It overwhelms people when they walk out the front and see them. *"What the Hell is That?"* It's like something from that scary old black-and-white movie, "The Birds." They are huge and look from a distance like harpy eagles when flying, but they are not.

## Harpy Eagles

Every year, I usually see a harpy eagle passing through. Very few people know that they come through here. There is a secret to identifying it as a harpy eagle, not a vulture. Those two are about the same size. Little birds go straight up at eagles.

In comparison, they may be smaller, but they harass all the raptor birds. Harpy eagles, hawks, and gyrfalcons get aggressive harassment. It happens because the little birds protect their babies in their nests. So, if birds harass a predator, it is not a vulture. It might be the rare sighting of a harpy eagle!

**ProTip:** Do not call for help, animal control, or the police when the *Black Squirrels* act up.

# Black Squirrel!

I urge you to know about the area's drunken black squirrel problem. It happens when the guava fruit falls and ferments in the warm sun. It is rare, but they know when the liquor runs for free. They all come to partake in the party under the guava tree at the end of my hotel's coffee shop's drive-thru.

They chatter like maniacs and wrestle with each other. They take crazy falls off the jacuzzi and the white fence surrounding the back terrace. Our German guests often fear they have rabies.

No kidding. Once, black squirrels stopped traffic in our drive-thru. A customer got out of their car to complain. "Senior! You have sick squirrels blocking the road." I had to ask those boozers to move along. They weren't sleeping; they were drunk and passed out in the drive-thru!

In summary, it is not rabid squirrel behavior. It is simple drunken squirrel behavior. The show includes short stunt-man falls and false chainsaw chattering charges at the crowds. They also wrestle with their mates until they are lying exhausted and semi-coherent. You should not interrupt or confuse spontaneous napping with sudden death. They are on the sauce and will be pretty OK tomorrow. But they're going to be a little *Hungover* or *Crudo.* That means you feel like *Raw Meat*.

Chapter 14

# Fun in Boquete

## Food with a Feeling

*Malu Cafe and Bakery:* +507-730-9251 - It is one of my favorite choices. Their second location in Central Park is where I love to write and have an excellent park-side breakfast. Finding the original location can be tricky; the park entry gate is sometimes closed. Malu serves up some delicious Gringo Style sausages for breakfast. I can't get enough of their generous meat platter.

*Chop Sticks A Restaurant:* +507-720-8416 - Best Egg Rolls Ever! Everything is lovely, but I love them so much that sometimes I order two sets of egg rolls and call it good. They treat you like family. They are part of mine.

*Retrogusto:* +507-6679-8028 - I love the owner (*Davide Carrera*) like a brother. He is married to the most beautiful woman in the village. (She always blushes when I say that) Their little girl is a happy dancing machine with water wings. Davide is Panama's Greatest Chef. You won't be disappointed. Everything is so delicious, and the service is excellent.

*Butcher Chophouse:* +507-6679-8028 - Tomahawk Steaks! They are enormous and tasty. He ages meat to perfection. Don't miss his variety tray of desserts. He has grass-fed and aged Panamanian steak filets for which to die. Check out the salt tray! It is another of *Davide's* Restaurants. Notice the semi-open seating area with a fireplace between these two restaurants.

*Riccos Pizzeria:* +507-6570-0517—They are opening a new location at the Caldera cutoff down at the Police Stop. I have taken hundreds of people to eat Iris's Calzone. Ask for extra sauce. I am excited about their reopening! Call ahead and get one to go on your way up, coming from David!

*Sabor Escondido (Hidden Flavor), Terra Lounge & La Cantina Bar:* +507-720-2454 - My friend *Thalía Velásquez-Taliaferro de Salazar* is the owner of *Valle Escondido Resort, Golf & Spa* in Bajo Boquete. I rented a villa there when I first arrived. She recently rebuilt the streamside *Sabor Escondido Restaurant.* I love the Brunch, Steaks, and everything else they do. Her team is outstanding! All three are inside Valle Escondido. *Terra Lounge* is the hidden jewel. It is vegan and kosher and is available only by reservation. It hides next to the indoor pool of the Spa. It has a Fireplace, a pool table, and incredible views! They have a Bone Broth Vegan Soup to die for. I love to work and take meetings there.

*Tacos Rudos:* +507-6233-9009 - Oh My God! Alejandro's food is Art! He is outgoing, bilingual and is from Mexico City. I did some of my undergrad there, and we are buddies. I love his fish tacos and *Queso Fundido (Melted Cheese)!* They are world-famous, no joke! It is hard to locate. Find it next door to the horse pasture west of Restaurant Row. Pick up the guava fruit from the ground at the restaurant and feed it to the horses afterward. I can't wait for his new Tex-Mex restaurant to open!

*Big Daddy's Grill:* +507-6250-1948 - Boom-Boom Chicken Salad! Wow! I almost bought this restaurant when I first got here. The Boom-Boom makes me wish I had. It has a lovely back area in the jungle with a big circle fire pit for fun on chilly nights.

*Tre Scalini Boquete:* +507-730-9255 - Sit in the back and take in the view. I sit on the street side to see all my buddies walking by. The owner and employees are friends. Their food is excellent. I don't know what they call it, but my favorite is the seafood linguini in a foil bag. Wow! That's delicious! Try the eggplant tower appetizer. It's wonderful.

*La Posada Boqueteña:* +507-730-9440—They make my favorite pizza in town. It is called *La Siciliana (The Sicilian).* They also have great nachos, steaks, and drinks of all kinds. I like the owner. He's an old cowboy like me but a real Argentine Gaucho.

*Tocoholics:* +507-6167-0547 - It is worth the short drive to the Los Naranjos neighborhood of Bajo Boquete. Sit outside and watch the goings-on in this old-fashioned neighborhood. The *Pibel (shredded pork)* Tacos are my favorites. I can't believe it. I'm a Tacoholic! Lol!

*El Sabrosón #1, 3 & 4:* All three are cafeteria style, low cost, and fresh. #1 is across from Multibank and you sit on picnic tables. #3 is on the southwest corner of central park. You sit at tables with chairs and chairs. It has a good view on the terrace. #4 is new, two stories, and on the main road in Alto Boquete. It has space for parties.

# Wonderful Coffee Shops

*Coffee Shop Don Nery:* +507-6660-0808- This coffee shop overlooks this steep valley farm. It has a great view of Volcan Baru. It is my newest discovery. They grow the coffee right there. It is a spectacular location with a scenic drive up to it. The owners are lovely people. I often order their *Batidos* (*Strawberry Milkshakes*) and coffee. They have great WiFi in the middle of nowhere. And eagles are nested nearby. They have many orchids displayed. They will soon pave their way to the entry of Volcan Baru National Park.

*Buckle Tip Coffee Studio:* +507-6965-3321 (Nair Batista-Barista/Manager), +507-6469-8591 (Manuel Burac - Barista/Manager) and +507-6227-4219 (Richard Cianca, Owner) - This is my home away from home. Meet their amazing baristas and try the best specialty coffee in the world. They spoil me with Focaccia sandwiches and Avocado toast. This coffee studio is perfect for people-watching and feeling the Boquete vibe. It is next to the big clock and fountains in Central Park. If you arrive by bus from David, it is ten steps away. Make them smile. Ask where *Tío Tim* is! Or say, "Where is the *Boquete Whisperer?*"

*Café Central:* +507-730-9676/+507-6103-2605 - If you're looking for an incredible view, Italian espresso drinks made with *Specialty Coffee (scoring 86-87 points)*, Hammocks, and Free Co-Working Space, this is the place for you. It is still the country's only Drive-Thru-Coffee! It is in the reception area of Boquete's #1 most popular (on Booking dot Com) hotel. Yep, it is still mine, *Hotel Central Boquete.* Try the BLT or Breakfast. Thank me later.
https://www.hotelcentralboquete.com/

*La Brûlerie:* +507-720-1111 - Get an exquisite cup of coffee on the 400-hectare farm. The friendly owners and employees adopted my *Uncle John,* so they are an extended family. This is your place if you want to bird watch or find a top birding guide and trails. It is hidden above the *Hotel and Coffee Farm Finca Lérida +507-833-7598.* Climb from the coffee shop (the best spot to photograph hummingbirds) to this hidden restaurant. It is up the hill with a lovely view and a new high-tech espresso machine. https://hotelfincalerida.com/.

*Boquete Sandwich Shop:* +507-730-9527 - It is a significant expat destination. Come early in the evening and enjoy their exquisite Caribbean Coconut Creamed Shrimp. They serve and sell the famous *Panama Joe Coffee:* +507-6878- 8962. Each bag is beautifully branded with a blue morpho butterfly. It is high-octane; you're going to fly out of there. Everything is delicious, but I've recently fallen in love with the cob salad.

*Sugar and Spice:* +507-730-9376 - Another great expat hangout. I love their Reuben sandwich. *Richard,* the owner and my friend is the hardest-working guy in the village. I love his cookies and bakery goods. Notice he has unlimited free ice water with real fruit juice in it. The coffee is great; get your refill on it. http://www.sugarandspiceboquete.com/

*Bambuda Castle:* +1-786-789-4889 - What a view! What a great cup of coffee! What nice people! It is the only Castle Hotel in Central America. I often work there as they have large tables on the balcony inside and outside. Be careful when the switchback road goes up. I like the pizza and chicken wings there as well. Bring new people there to experience it. https://bambuda.com/castle/

*Morton's Bakehouse:* +507-730-8449 - It is Kosher and owned by my friend, the *Hasidic Rabbi Jacob.* I don't know where to start. They have gluten-free options. Enjoy fantastic bagels made up how you like them. They have super delicious coffee. And what a garden! You can sit inside or out! Notice the happy baking crew singing and dancing three steps away. It's an excellent place to meet people. I am editing this book now in the large, serene garden in the back. This link, https://mortonsbakehouse.com/story/, will take you to their backstory. The founder, Morton, was a friend of mine. I am happy that Chabad Boquete and Morton merged to continue his legacy.

## Great Hiking

*Pipeline Trail* - A flat, easy to moderate difficulty path. It is home to the most enormous tree in Provence and a great waterfall at the end. Homeland of the Resplendent Quetzal Bird.

*The Three Lost Waterfalls Trail* - Steep, moderate to difficult and slippery in the wet season. +507-6691-9144

*Finca Lérida* - Best Private Birding Trail and Birding Guides. https://hotelfincalerida.com/

*Boquete Library Riverside Park* - Hike from the library one block to the River Park. Enter when it opens, at 6:00 a.m.and go from starlight to first light to sunlight. You will love it! https://www.biblioboquete.com/

*Paseo del Río (River Walk)* - This trail passes under and connects to the Panamonte Bridge on the east side of the river. It is lit up at night, has good seating, and is currently being extended on both ends.

## Take a Tour or Day Trip

These are a sample from years of feedback from my friends and hotel customers.

*Iwanna Boquete Tours:* +507-6676-1150 - *Coffee and Nature* - I love *Lan's* passion. He is funny and friendly. The coffee farm you go to, *Don Pepe Estate,* is owned by a pair of brothers. Their grandpa set it up, and it is picturesque. All three are my friends. The tour is impressive and very educational! And you drink *Geisha Coffee!* Our Geisha is the most expensive coffee in the world. https://iwannaboquetetours.com/

*Boquete Outdoor Adventures:* +507-720-2284 - *Jim*, the owner, is my friend; he also came from Montana. They do it all. River Rafting,

Hiking, Whale watching, Birding, Island trips, and Coffee Tours. Check out their "Best of Boquete" three-day package. https://www.boqueteoutdooradventures.com/

*Boquete Bees and Butterflies:* +507-720-2939/+507-6446-5654 - *Emily* has a coffee shop now! I love everything there! There is so much to do. Don't miss the *Butterfly House!* And pick up some of her amazing *Honey.* Her tours are a once-in-a-lifetime experience. https://www.natureboquete.com/

*Horseback Riding:* +507-6734-1106/+507-6510-9653 - Great horses in a beautiful place. It is unforgettable. *Rudy* and his family are pure fun. Their horses are gentle and well cared for.

*Beyond Adventures Tours:* +507-6130-1414 - They do it all. Summit Volcan Baru. They have guided hikes. Go river rafting. Enjoy horseback riding. Private transfers to Bocas del Toro-Panama City-Airport-Paso Canoas. Rappelling! Island day tours in the Gulf of Chiriqui. They have hot springs and mini canyon trips. The owner Rolando loves my coffee, is a friend, and his team does a great job. https://www.beyondadventuretours.com/

*4x4 to the Top of Volcano Baru:* +507-6539-3617 - Lan Miranda has awesome vehicles. He is a bit of a DJ with great tunes for the ride. He is Dr. Luz's husband and his nickname is *MacGyver.* You have got to see him climb up the towers on top.He has been maintaining the many telecom's installations for decades. Go up as smooth as a cat climbing a tree. Leave the work to someone else. Be at the summit just before dawn. Clouds often block the view 15 - 20 minutes after sunrise. Bring a camera and all your warm clothes. You will need them! It can be freezing at the top.

*Las Lajas Beach Resort:* +507-6790-1972 - Hey there! If you're looking for a local gem, this beach is the place to be—perfect waves for body surfing, an hour and thirty-five minutes from paradise. You'll love the flat, safe shores for strolls. They have tasty food, boogie boarding, and poolside lounging. Enjoy the shady palapas, outdoor showers, and yummy treats. Whenever I need a break, this spot is my top pick. https://laslajasbeachresort.com/

*Playa Barqueta: (David Area)* - Barqueta Beach is the closest beach to the Provincial Capital, David. It is 40 minutes away from David. Go for the seafood, not for the swimming. I like eating at the far left restaurant (looking at the ocean). They have cold drinks and fresh fried *Pargo (Snapper)*. They are famous for their riptides that cause many drownings. It is an excellent place to walk on the beach.

*Check TripAdvisor:* Are you looking for some other ideas? Jump over to *Trip Advisor* and find out what is hot and what is not. Zoom out and check out the whole Province as well. https://www.tripadvisor.com/

*One-Day Tour in the Highland Area of Volcan*

(Leave early and do all three!)

*Barriles Archaeological Site (Sitio Barriles):* +507-6575-1828 -This location is one of the most famous archaeological sites in Panama. It has a great little museum, excavations, food, and drinks. It is worth checking out. The site is Open Daily from 7 a.m. to 6 p.m. The friendly owners have done an excellent job preserving and presenting the site.

*Raquel's Ark:* +507-6466-9530/ +1-786-598-0045 - "Rescuing exotic animals one at a time." I'm sad to report that Rachel is no longer with us. I am friends with all the animals and the incredible lady who owned, ran, and lived onsite. I liked my time with her, hugging sloths and playing with rare monkeys. Her big cat was scary. I hope someone steps in to keep it going because it's a favorite stop for grown-ups and children.

*Finca Dracula:* +507-771-2070 - Open daily 9:00 a.m. to 3:00 p.m. This beautiful location is a private Botanical Garden specializing in cultivating and conserving *over 2000 orchid species* From Central and South America. They are famous for growing *Dracula orchids.* Their Property is incredible. Don't miss it. Folks who love orchids go nuts here. https://fincadracula.com/

*Viajes David Travel Agency:* +507-720-2848/+507-6613-0595 - Go see Anavilma if you are looking for something fun to do. Her office

is in Bajo Boquete next to the lower river bridge.
vdavidtravel@gmail.com

*Get a Haircut at RS Barber Shop:* +507-6877-9780 - Ask for José Carlos. Google for the location and get a great haircut for $6!

Chapter 15
# The Rarest Rainbows

## Double, Triple, and Full Rainbows

When you visit here, get ready for a real treat. You'll see double rainbows, triple, and even full rainbows. They'll stack them on each other, stretching from earth to the heavens. It's unbelievable! And, thanks to the warm, wet Caribbean breeze, it's often misty here in Boquete. So we can get a jubilee of both morning and afternoon rainbows.

All you need is sunshine over your shoulder to complete the perfect picture with a vivid rainbow! Our valley's frequent sunshine mist has a nickname, *Bajareque*. It is at its height of activity in the windy, dry season. The locals call it a *Norte* because Strong winds blow from the north.

## Round Rainbows

About a year ago, I was fortunate to witness something special - a *Circular* or *Round Rainbow*. I sat in a cave full of baby frogs beneath my friend's waterfall on his new farm. It was quite a spiritual experience. I was skinny dipping then. I'll always remember how I lucked into seeing it.

I'd gotten a great massage from the warm water pounding on my back. But after climbing through the falls and frogs into a tiny cave behind me, I turned, sat, and looked out. And I saw it. A perfect Panamanian *Round Rainbow!*

What a remarkable world we live in! Moments like these make me appreciate nature's wonders. Who knew there was such a thing? But think back. How about running through the water sprinkler on hot summer days as a kid? Do you remember seeing how it can create round rainbows?

# Moon Rainbows

Boquete has a big secret. It's like a rainbow in front of you, the sun on your back. It's our Moon Rainbows. They're like the standard sun rainbows. The magnified moon's light forms them as the full moon sets. High humidity here can magnify and make the moon look enormous when it is full. It happens at night before the moon sets behind Volcano Baru to the west of us.

You must have the moon side clear, with a star-filled sky an hour or so before the coming dawn's first morning light. The pre-dawn mist must be super-fine and thick as heavy honey fog on the east side of the valley. That's the morning-shaded, chilly side of the valley. Sunny mornings bake the valley's west side. That leaves it warmer until the next dawn. That is why less mist forms on the western side to block a setting full moon, soon to hide behind the volcano.

At the start, to the east, on the opposite side of our volcano, the Moon-Rainbow emerges. At first, it sure looked like the luminescence of swamp gas I had seen in Oklahoma. I saw it while attending High School with Osage Native students. They lived east of the Arkansas River on the Osage Indian Reservation. These were glowing swamps and ponds beside hayfields near their many oil fields at night. Well, that *Moon-Rainbow* was a wonderful thing.

That's what it looked like. It was a scary moment. I thought our volcano was acting up, producing a glowing volcanic gas bubble. It was hanging low over the valley to the east. Over fifteen minutes, it rose and formed a rainbow in the darkness of night. *Moon Rainbows* can only form before the first light of dawn. It helps to be near no street or house lights. Turn them off or move far away if you can. That is what you do.

Wait for the unique giant full moon nights with a *Norte* or north wind. Sit in complete darkness for 15 - 20 minutes. That makes your eyes more sensitive. Seek pre-dawn clear skies to the west with the moon and fine mist on the east. Let your eyes adjust. You might see the elusive *Moon Rainbow*. Note: It is so hard to see that my camera could not pick it up!

# Fire Rainbows

Our *Fire Rainbows* are as rare as the luminescent, blue balls of *Saint Elmo's Fire* dancing down a barbed wire fence. I saw it one stormy night with my best friend and his mom in seventh grade. It was east of Ponca City, Oklahoma, at their country home. Seeing is believing. Please look up my photos (and friend me!) on Facebook. Use these search terms. First, enter my full first and last name, *Timothy Zellmer*. Second, type in *Fire Rainbows*. But enter the symbol: "+" after my name. Hit search to retrieve my photos.

*Fire Rainbows* are akin to *SunDogs* and *MoonDogs*. That is because the light source (Sun or Moon) and the rainbow effect are in the same direction. Remember, during regular rainbows, the light is on your back. The rainbow is in the opposite direction. Sundogs and *MoonDogs* are short pieces of rainbow that form on the right and left sides of the sun or moon. They're like colorful dogs on the left and right.

Please stay with me. I'm going to explain *Fire Rainbows*. It often freezes up there because Volcano Baru is tall (11,398 feet or 3474 meters). The hot, humid breeze arrives from Bocas del Toro Province, on the northern Caribbean side of the country. That builds up a thunderhead high above the summit of our volcano. Thunderheads are often anvil-shaped.

Scientists explain that thunderheads are dangerous cumulonimbus clouds. The tallest of these occur in the tropics. That is where Panama is. Their powerful updraft winds can reach 100 miles an hour. Scientists have recorded these towering formations as high as 75,000 feet! That is more than 14 miles high! They only get those heights in the hot, energetic tropics. At that soaring altitude, the water phase changes into ice crystals. As crystals, they act as a prism. That separates the sun's light into all the colors of the rainbow.

When the thunderheads rise over our Volcano Barú, they begin to block the late afternoon sun. Then, faster winds at the top of the cloud blow off the ice crystals. They fly to the left, or the south side, of the thunderhead. They fall in a cascading effect, looking like multi-colored plasma. That is where you'll start to see our fabled *Fire Rainbows*. They are a wonder to behold.

Recently, millions of people saw an enormous *Fire Rainbow* near Chicago. That one was different from ours. It was a saucer-shaped formation. Pictures of that one are easy to search for. But ours is the rarest of Fire Rainbows. It is waterfall-shaped. There is nothing quite like it. It's a waterfall coming off the top of a thunderhead made of rainbows!

Chapter 16
# Great Travel Hub

## Trips to the U.S. Embassy

Suppose you need to go to the U.S. Embassy in Panama City and don't want to spend on airline tickets. Take the new double-decker Mercedes buses between David and Panama City. They cost half a million bucks. It's an affordable and adventurous 6-7 hour trip for 20 bucks! But get ready for the bus to have some chilly temps, so bring a jacket or blanket. https://pa.usembassy.gov/

## Easy Costa Rican Getaways

Are you looking to get to Costa Rica from David, Panama, on the cheap? By bus, it'll take about an hour and run you an excellent $2.25 to reach the border crossing at *Paso Canoas*. But wait, there's more! If you need to get to *San Jose*, the capital of *Costa Rica,* you're looking at a seven-hour journey that will cost you $18 more.

Many people take advantage of sweet deals on international flights. I'm talking about the flights leaving from and returning to the Costa Rican capital, San José. Get to Juan Santamaría International Airport (SJC is the city code) and leave. Take a look at the flights offered by *Spirit Air* in Costa Rica. You save a bunch of money that way. https://www.spirit.com/

We have a contingency of retired expats who rent out their homes during our noisy holiday season. They travel by bus to San José, Costa Rica, and take cheap flights to *Mexico City*. They take a small bus to *San Miguel de Allende, Mexico*. It is a community of artists. Like Boquete, it is on the list of the *100 most beautiful villages in the world*. https://www.visitsanmiguel.travel/

## Discover Columbia on the Cheap

Hey there! Are you looking for fantastic travel deals to Colombia? Get ready for an unforgettable adventure! Dive into the fantastic culture, lively cities, and stunning landscapes. The warmth of the Colombian people and the mouthwatering cuisine are incredible. Colombia has everything you need, whether you're into historical sites, pristine beaches, or exciting outdoor activities.

And guess what? It's super affordable, giving you incredible value for your travel budget. Oh, and did I mention that it's also known for being safe and clean? So, explore with peace of mind. Take advantage of this incredible opportunity to discover the wonders of Colombia! https://colombia.travel/en

# Travel Inside Panama

Are you planning to explore all the wonders of Panama? Get ready for an unforgettable journey! This place has something for everyone. It has lush jungles, stunning beaches, and vibrant cities. Plus, it has a rich, unique culture. And remember the mouthwatering food - it will satisfy you! Plus, it's more affordable compared to Costa Rica.

Whether you're up for an adventure or want to unwind, let me tell you, Panama is a great place to live. Start planning your trips today. You better get ready. The magic of Panama will enchant you! It's a world unto itself. https://www.tourismpanama.com/

# 10 Great Places to Visit in Panama

*Panama City* - Towering skyscrapers contrast with charming historic colonial buildings. Walk along her *Cinta Costera (Coast Ribbon)* public recreation space. It is 4.3 miles (7 km) in length. Check out the *Metropolitan National Park*, a real gem covering 654.8 acres (265 hectares). It's nestled in the multifaceted *Ancón* district. It is the only protected area in Central America in an urban setting. Visit the *Biomuseo* and the *Miraflores Locks* of the 51-mile (82-kilometer) long Panama Canal. Discover *Soberania National Park, which is* only 15 miles away from downtown.

https://es.tourismpanama.com/lugares-para-visitar/ciudad-de-panama/

*Casco Viejo* - Whichmeans *Old Town* in Spanish, is a fantastic historic district in Panama City. It's got all these old buildings, streets made of cobblestones, and a super lively vibe. You've got tradition mixed with modern stuff going on. You won't believe the marketplace there. It's bustling with street food, crafts, and everything representing Panama's incredible culture. Oh, and in the evening, you must check out the fountains. They've got these sunset views that will take your breath away.
https://www.tourismpanama.com/places-to-visit/panama-city/casco-antiguo/

*Boquete* - Discover the allure. Hit the trails. Charm meets majestic mountains and lush coffee plantations here. Embark on thrilling adventures like zip-lining and rock climbing. Soak in our nearby hot springs. And take advantage of the opportunity to savor the finest coffee in the world. Don't miss the Flower and Coffee Fair or the Boquete Jazz and Blues Festival.
https://www.tourismpanama.com/places-to-visit/boquete/

*El Valle de Anton* - This highland caldera-formed valley is a picture-perfect village! It's got lively markets and a mesmerizing volcanic crater. There's tons of biodiversity. The museums will leave you spellbound, and the gardens are charming. You can also enjoy exhilarating hikes to soothing hot springs. Explore this heavenly paradise and find rare orchids and golden frogs. It's something special! https://www.tourismpanama.com/places-to-visit/cocle/anton-valley/

*Santa Catalina*- It's a fabulous fishing village that surfers and scuba divers love! It's famous for having the best waves in that slice of the country. You can't miss the breathtaking diving opportunities at Coiba National Park. Oh, and did I mention the incredible sunsets over the ocean? They're unforgettable!
https://es.tourismpanama.com/lugares-para-visitar/costa-pacifica-de-veraguas/santa-catalina/

*The Pearl Islands* - These are very charming islands! Picture yourself in this Pacific paradise. Pristine white sand and stunning

turquoise waters surround you. Get close to magnificent whales, playful dolphins, and graceful sea turtles. Immerse yourself in the wonders of nature. That's an experience you won't want to miss!
https://www.tourismpanama.com/places-to-visit/panama/pearl-islands/

*Bocas del Toro*- This area has aCaribbean coastal archipelago with thousands of stunning islands. It has Great Beaches and snorkeling, like something from the movie *Avatar!* I flew with flocks of baby squid! There are two certified dive schools. Surfers get unique experiences, getting dropped off mid-channel with their surfboard to catch great waves between the islands and ride to the beach. Take a tour of Indigenous communities like Salt Creek. It's great to get in touch with local culture. They have *Red Frogs and Lion Fish.* Don't touch them. They are both poisonous.
https://www.tourismpanama.com/places-to-visit/bocas-del-toro/

*Playa Venao* - This spot is a renowned destination for backpackers and surfers worldwide. Find pristine beaches and world-class waves at this beach town. There's something for everyone, whether you're a seasoned surfer or a laid-back backpacker. Hit the beach, feel the vibes of the culture, and bask in the sun in this coastal paradise!
https://es.tourismpanama.com/que-hacer/playas/playas-populares/playa-venao/

*Guna Yala* - You must visit once in your life. This Caribbean Indigenous Autonomous Homeland is heaven on earth. This archipelago experience is top-notch. It has tropical islands with a blend of traditional and modern tribal cultures. It is in a class all by itself. The tribe's warmth and friendliness are well-known. These protected lands are its ancestral homeland.
https://es.tourismpanama.com/que-hacer/comunidades-indigenas/guna/

*Coiba* - Coiba Island and the smaller neighboring islands are offshore in the Pacific Ocean in the Gulf of Chiriqui. They have a past as a former penal colony. This remarkable diving destination is one of the world's most diverse. Experience encounters with Manta Rays, Whales, and Hammerhead Sharks. It also features stunning beaches and vibrant coral reefs, which complete the allure of this extraordinary place. https://es.tourismpanama.com/naturaleza-y-parques/parques-nacionales/parque-nacional-isla-coiba/

Chapter 17

# Geographic Arbitrage

## Panama's Super Powers of Geographic Arbitrage

You say, "What is Geographic Arbitrage?" The basic definition is taking advantage of the cost differences between two locations. It can mean earning in a *strong currency* and then spending using a *weaker currency*. Earn your money in a *strong economy,* but pay it in a *weaker economy.* The idea is to retire somewhere you gain leverage. This can significantly speed up the time it takes you to achieve financial independence.

Many people use geographic arbitrage to retire early. Often, U.S. citizens continue working to maintain good health insurance, so retirement is out of reach. They are working to avoid $1,500/month (or more) health insurance premiums. It can feel frustrating, like a trap. There is an emerging rush of people looking at international retirement opportunities worldwide.

Okay, let me break it down for you. Most people think it's only about money. Go for the easy. Take advantage of the low-hanging fruit locations in the world when making money. But spend it where it stretches the farthest. Geographic arbitrage is about the many ways you can take advantage of *location.* The cost of living, taxes, and other factors differ depending on your spot. But it's not only about money. And this is where things start to get interesting.

Folks get fixated on cost savings alone. It's essential to think about quality of life, too. Consider things like the weather. How about security and infrastructure? And recreational opportunities. How friendly is the local population? We gather up happy people here. Few places are as welcoming as Boquete.

The community has been mixing since it was founded 113 years ago. Many Panamanian students attend universities in other countries. Those kids might fall in love there. They get married. Their kids speak many languages. They work outside Panama for part of their lives. Then they come home. They know how to use geographic arbitrage.

Consider how easy it is to socialize and make friends. This factor alone can yield a vast improvement in your life's quality. You can start ahead in the retirement game by changing your location on Earth. There is a great deal of information online about hotspots. The best places for international retirement worldwide.

## Retirement Visa Program

Let's take Panama, for instance. It has its famous retirement visa program, super low taxes, and a good standard of living—standards that are way better than many other countries. So, Panama is a good choice if you want to get more for your money without sacrificing quality of life. You can save some serious cash by tapping into these price differences. You can still enjoy the same goodies and services while being in a happier, better place—better in many ways.

Remember Panama's business-friendly laws. They make setting up companies a breeze, resulting in even more tax savings. Many factors make Panama ideal. It's an excellent spot for people looking for geographic arbitrage opportunities. Sounds good.

## Panama has Max-Leverage

Alright, let's talk about economic leverage in Panama. Panama is not cheap, but it's reasonable. You won't suffer here if your retirement budget makes you seek a *more affordable cost of living.* One thing that makes Panama stand out is its *Retirement Visa.* It offers discounts beyond what you'd find in any other country. It's one of a kind and beats everything else out there. Of course, housing costs can vary depending on location and size. But generally speaking, Panama's housing is affordable.

The best part is that *Panama uses U.S. dollars.* That's helpful if you're, like most of us, holding U.S. dollars; there's *no need to hassle with currency exchange.* And here's another great thing:

120

Panamanians and legal residents receive *public healthcare.* Plus, *public transportation* is cheap and almost everywhere. So, you've got a lot of financial positives going for you when you choose Panama!

Next, let's look at leveraging Panama's fantastic *environmental benefits.* Trust me, it's not a filthy country at all! It's pretty clean, green, and oh-so-beautiful. You'll always have easy access to stunning beaches, islands, and lush forests here. And let me tell you, whale watching is an absolute must-do! Panama is where baby dolphins come to be born.

> *ProTip*: Attention all SCUBA divers! Water visibility is at its peak for five months of the year. Plan your scuba diving from mid-December to mid-April.

I had an incredible offshore fishing trip off the Pacific Coast of Chiriqui Province. Three pods of overly friendly baby dolphins decided to join us for the entire day. It was a magical experience! I never caught so many fish. We filled up all the ice chests and the live hold. We had so many, and we gave them to the ladies who cook at the gravel bar boat launch at *Boca Chica/ Boca Brava.*

Don't forget to visit *Starfish Beach* and *Sloth Island* in the Bocas del Toro Province's islands. They're incredible! The country has more than 1,600 islands off its Atlantic and Pacific coasts. Take time for magical snorkeling in the rich marine life-filled mangroves. That's so inspiring. In Panama, nature's beauty is at its finest. You'll feel like you're living in paradise.

You'll never catch a blizzard in Panama, so there's no need to hold onto your snow shovels and blowers. But grab a large umbrella. The rain tends to come straight down, usually arriving late afternoon. One of the great things about living here is the variety of nearby weather options. You don't have that in most places.

# Too cold or raining cats and dogs?

If it's raining in Boquete, you can always head down to Caldera's hot springs For a short hike and a soak. It's likely to be clear and warm down there. It's only about 45 minutes away. Use this simple strategy. Too chilly? Head downhill. Too hot? Head uphill.

Panama is such a special place! It's a narrow strip of land surrounded by vast oceans. The air here feels fresh and pure, and you won't find noisy planes filling the sky. Seeing one in the highlands is quite a sight - everyone stops to admire it! And let me tell you, rare birds and butterflies are a part of our everyday scenery.

So, picture songbirds singing outside your window. Visit from flocks of little green parrots. They are your neighbors. Go riverside and see beautiful Cranes, Plovers, and Cara Cara Eagles flying by daily. Oh, and have I mentioned the Boquete Library Park? It's home to over 20 turtles. I spotted a large new one this morning. It is a type that I've never seen before. Panama is a place of awe and wonder!

Finally, Look at the leverage you get by living in a relaxed, friendly, safe place. Panama is *Muy Tranquilo!* That means it's very tranquil. Many expatriates have been able to get off medication. They do so much better with blood pressure, anxiety, and sleeping. I've had so many clients at the hotel tell me they've never slept better than they have here. You can finally relax. Hypervigilance begins to fade. There are countless combat veterans living here for that reason.

I don't know where it comes from, but there's this saying about leverage. "If you've got a long enough lever, you can move the Moon." It's a fantastic way to think about Geographic Arbitrage. And that brings me to something I want to share.

## Use Geographic Arbitrage to Increase Your Neuroplasticity.

*Neuroplasticity* is one of the areas of study of the brain. It focuses on how the brain changes and adapts. Neuroplasticity is the opposite of what I learned in school about the brain. That your brain could only decay and never heal itself. Scientists have discovered that that's not true.

The brains of *Newcomers* here transform. You are changing because stress hormones are decreasing. You are spending more time outside. You are in nature and eating better. You are also making more social connections. It's something you can witness here daily. People seem more relaxed, less "on edge," and more present. They become new people—a better version of themselves.

Imagine this: the brain is an incredible organ. It connects our visual cortex (where the brain sees) through our eyes. Anatomists now consider the eyes to be the external extension of the brain. Mind-blowing, right? Scientists studying this have a fascinating hypothesis. There is an interconnectedness between our brain's functions and the eyes. Learn more from *Dr. Huberman* at the *Huberman Lab Podcast*.

They believe changing our environment can rewire our minds in as little as three weeks. It's pretty fascinating stuff! They've found spending time in nature does it. Contact with a green light creates positive rewiring of the brain. More social interactions also have this effect. Panama has plenty of all three. Intense exposure to nature, green, and socializing here will fix your brain.

Immerse yourself. These transformative experiences happen every day by simply being here. We've got stunning greenery all around. You will saturate your eyes with green light. You will have the most incredible nature experiences. You're going to have lots of opportunities to meet cheerful folks. Everyone is up for a chat. Those same brain scientists say that *mood is catchy!* By hanging out with happy, relaxed people, your brain starts running that way!

## Green is Good

Shockingly, those neuroscientists I mentioned found that green light can rewire our brains. It leads to a happier state and makes you feel less pain. Believe it or not, it *gives you greater strength*. People can walk farther. People get out more. Vitamin D levels hit healthy levels. Arthritis improves. You feel less achy. What's not to like about that?

Get your treatments right here. I notice massive changes in *Newcomers*. We all see significant improvements in people's happiness. I have come to understand that there are waypoints to these dramatic improvements. Take note of the difference at four days, four months, and four years. You can become almost unrecognizable. People change that much.

So, why not treat yourself to a bit of transformation? Get to Boquete, Panama, and take a walk in paradise. You can relax, feel secure, and enjoy the lovely climate. You can also connect with a community that values friendship, peace, and respect. You will soon see it happen. This place changes people. It changes you for the better.

## How Acceptance Leads to Geographic Arbitrage

Some say *Acceptance is the Key to your Serenity*. Too many people live in a distortion field. Open yourself up to the concept of geographic arbitrage. People stay in the wrong places for them. Things change, and they don't. Nobody likes to make a choice. You can completely change your life by deciding to move. And guess what? That's what I did!

I had a tough time accepting how I'd changed. I was a lousy match for where I was living in Montana. Panama was a wake-up call for me and made me realize things. Back then, in Montana, my doctors ganged up on me. They forced me to look at things I didn't want to. I went kicking and screaming till the end. They stole the dental drill and the reins of my horses from my two hands. My prescription was not too hot, not too cold, zero stress. Go where you feel better.

**Pro Tip:** To maintain your motivation in tasks, remember the *Goldilocks Rule* from "Atomic Habits" by James Clear - *not too easy, not too hard*. This principle keeps you consistently driven in both life and work.

Put yourself back in the place of Goldilocks and the Three Bears. She saw and accepted that she loved a specific temperature of her breakfast porridge. She didn't like it to be too hot or too cold.

Through experience, she identified what was best for her. She wanted it to be *just right*. She rejected the others. She found what was *right* for her. And so should you.

You've got a question? How many times did she eat porridge that was too hot or too cold before she decided not to do that anymore? *Denial isn't Some River in Egypt*, my friend. *If you don't know what you want, how will you ever get it?* Also, what you don't want. I didn't want to fight the horrible shakes of hypothermia from my weakened heart in the winters of Montana. My spine couldn't handle falling on black ice. I bet this resonates with some of you. Think about what you would enjoy avoiding. And that will keep you going forward.

Chapter 18
# Three Methods for Relocating to Boquete

## Look Before You Leap

You know that famous saying, *Look before you leap*? It's like a friendly reminder. Take a moment before making any major decision, such as moving to Boquete. The saying is a wise metaphor. It compares decision-making to a leap into the unknown. And you know what? Looking first helps avoid potential dangers that might come after that big decision.

You're pretty smart. You're reading this book and checking out my videos and other people's stuff online. It's a way to get a sneak peek into life here. But you must watch out for that thing called delusion. Here, we call it *Panamá Loco (Crazy Panama)*. Our minds and hearts can play tricks on us. We get so caught up in the idea of this place. Start building it up to be this perfect kind of thing. And boy, does that set us up for a major letdown.

It is wise to come here and get a feel for life. It's worth investing a week or two. Experience is the best teacher, you know? I've seen many people who planned to stay for a month or even longer. It took them only a little while to figure out the upsides and downsides of living their dream life here. They also considered how it could align with their goals. I sometimes warn these folks. *"You're swimming in the deep end without water wings!"* You may not escape Boquete. Or even want to!

## The Snowbird Option

Canadians like the snowbird option more than citizens of any other country. Recently, they are starting to choose to live here year-round. Snowbirds are here, escaping the cold for six months. Then, they return home for six months. Many have homes in both locations. One reason they do that is to avoid losing Canadian Healthcare Insurance. They must live in Canada for six months, plus a day, every year. Check with your Attorney. I can't tell you about that.

You know what's interesting? During the rainy season, some folks leave Panama. Can you believe it? It's beautiful here. It's called the green season. But let's be honest. Most people prefer to dodge the cold season up north instead. Do you stay for Christmas? Do you leave after New Year's? And do you know what makes driving away from the cold more complex? Or if you have grandkids, they are more available during summer break.

So, they shape their Snowbird lifestyle around these issues, you know? I've heard from plenty of grandparents who now live here. They're spending way more time with their grandkids. Their children drop off the little ones and have a blast traveling around Panama. That's different from what they expected. It's a pleasant surprise!

Some people can afford to keep their options open. It's fascinating how everything, from health to family to finances, needs to line up right. I know quite a few folks who have second or even third homes. They keep them for their annual get-togethers with their friends and family. These people are at that incredible stage of life, prioritizing making memories. They get together in stunning places, surrounded by their loved ones.

# Burn Your Boat

If you burn your boat, you'll take the islands. There's no retreat if you sell everything, including the house, cars, and the whole shebang, Then arrive here thinking you'll be here forever. And it's your first visit. You *Burned Your Boat!* It is a risky way to get here. If you are aggressive and decisive, that could be you. Of course, this is not so risky if you speak Spanish and are a world traveler. You cannot keep looking back and thinking about what you left behind. You have to look ahead and make the best of it. You've chosen full adventure mode.

You are now in this beautiful place with a new way of life. Get involved in the local community. Make friends who share your values and interests. Work hard if necessary and learn how to enjoy life and relax. You burned your boat so that you won't sail away anytime soon.

This option is neither good nor bad. Have you traveled the world with your career? Have you lived in many countries? This might be the perfect fit for you. But it can lead to awful outcomes for folks without life experiences like that. I've seen people bounce out of Panama faster than a ricochet bullet! I've seen cases where people left before their cargo container, which was full of all their stuff, even arrived. And that can be pretty darn hard and expensive.

Chapter 19

# Panamanians Love Boquete

## Panamanian Kids - Crazy About Boquete!

I ask the littlest Panamanian kids what they think about Boquete. Their response? Pure magic! They paint a picture of blooming flowers, aromatic coffee, and lively parades! And that it is so cold here! It is not Montana cold, but it is the popular chilly spot of Panama.

Youngsters often describe Boquete as a charming little village. They remember it for its vibrant display of colorful flowers. It's fresh brewed coffee aroma. It is exciting parades and festivals. They all hope to join our parades with their school's marching band. Notice the variety of names on the many school buses! They come from all over. It unlocks the chance for the country's youth to represent their town on the exciting stage of Boquete.

You should see how pumped up kids get when they arrive here. They leap out of the car. They immediately hug their moms, dads, aunties, or grandmas. They come dressed in traditional Panamanian attire like *La Pollera*. The pollera is a traditional Panamanian dress, often adorned with exquisite gold jewelry. People wear it during festive occasions, symbolizing nationalism and folklore. This attire is a testament to the rich cultural heritage. It emerged when Spanish conquerors first set foot on this land.

The sweet fragrance of mountain flowers fills the air. Smell the delicious grilled snacks from the street vendors. You can't resist trying them out. Let's not forget their sheer joy of seeing a nearby waterfall. *Cascada San Ramon,* or Saint Raymond's Falls, is north of town. It's all part of the excitement!

For many Panamanians, celebrating life's simple pleasures is a must. Every day, the streets of Boquete come alive with laughter, music, and dancing. Locals work together to give kids beautiful, lasting memories. Their smiles and laughter will warm your soul even on our chill nights.

## Burning Desire in Young Adults

Young adults dream of a grandparent moving (So they can sofa-surf) or getting a job here. They all want to visit or live in Boquete! The experience here is a rare treat that not everyone in her bustling cities enjoys. It includes magnificent, panoramic vistas of majestic mountains. There are also charming and cozy coffee shops and bakeries.

It breaks my heart to see the struggles young Panamanians face. It's hard for them to move and chase their dreams here. Adapting to a different environment and trying to establish themselves can be overwhelming. They inspire with their resilience and determination to overcome these obstacles.

The path to success and stability may not be smooth, but they remind us that we can all overcome challenges and achieve our goals. Young City-Dwelling Adults yearn to move to Boquete.

## Where Panamanian Retirees Want To End Up

I spoke with a friend from Panama City who told me he bought two hectares here and is building a home. He is not the only Panamanian moving here after retirement; there are many new ones now.

It's easy to get here. Everyone enjoys our enhanced connectivity. Panamanians of retirement age love the new roads. It has cut travel time and improved safety. We had years of enduring longer travel times, guide cars, and rerouted roadways. They have finally completed the Pan-American Highway. They also finished the road between David and Boquete. These roads are not an improvement. They've been a complete game-changer for the region.

It has become even more convenient for families to visit. And for those looking to retire in Boquete, the improved road access is a blessing. It adds to the allure of the region. It also enhances the living experience in this picturesque part of Panama. They now have easy access to our great climate.

Panamanian Retirees want to live in Boquete. It is a beautiful town nestled amidst lush mountain greenery. They think like the rest of us - they find this place remarkable! Its breathtaking landscapes, pleasant climate, and welcoming community make it an appealing destination.

It's ideal for those facing retirement. Panama's Department of Tourism recently completed a research project. They identified the seven top tourist destinations. Guess what! Boquete is number one on their list. Everyone they know will want to visit! Lol! The serene beauty of Boquete entices Panamanian people from all walks of life. They dream of making it their home sweet home.

Chapter 20
# Tips and Tricks for Paradise

## Best Tech Practices

Go Heavy on these Apps:

- *Waze:* Your go-to navigation buddy, ensuring you never miss a turn and smoothly guiding you to your destination hassle-free.
- *Duolingo:* Dive into learning a new language and become a language enthusiast, or expand your linguistic horizons with engaging lessons.
- *Google Translate:* The ultimate tool for seamless communication, whether you're shopping globally or navigating different languages effortlessly.
- *Trip Advisor:* Are you curious about a new place? Check out reviews to make informed decisions and make the most of your experiences.
- *Google Maps:* Learn about your surroundings. Notice the many clickable links on Google Maps.
- App Boquete: A Business Directory - Community Resource - Travel Guide. Save the link. It is super handy and provides an insider's view to what is happening here now.

Avoid these Apps:

- *Google or Apple Maps for Navigation:* Instead, use more specialized local apps that cater to your specific area for enhanced navigation and seamless communication. Users have filled Waze with local knowledge. You can uncover hidden gems, get more accurate directions, and connect more effectively within your local community.

The Only Way to Communicate

- *WhatsApp:* WhatsApp is the go-to choice when chatting in Panama or sending your location. From setting up group chats to sharing the latest buzz, folks in Panama count on WhatsApp for all their communication tasks. https://www.whatsapp.com/download

## Beachside Wellness

Little-Known Treatments:

- *Listerine:* To prevent swimmer's ear after beach water exposure, a helpful tip is to apply a few drops of Blue Listerine in each ear. Any flavor would do, but I like the blue one better. Gently swab and dry the ears with Q-Tips for effective results.
- *Sunscreen and Bug spray:* When heading out, apply sunscreen before bug spray. This will provide optimal protection against harmful UV rays and insects, and bug juice.
- *1% Cortisone cream:* In case of bug bites, immediately apply 1% Cortisone cream to alleviate itching and inflammation.
- *Triple Antibiotic Cream:* This is for added relief and to avoid an infection at the bite on your skin. You apply a triple antibiotic cream on the bites before bedtime to promote healing overnight.

## Matters of the Heart

- Navigating Relationships:
- Beware of the allure of engaging romantically with others online. They are in a tropical paradise, while you are not.
- Focus on the practical parts of moving for retirement. Don't seek romance with those who may not be your economic equals. They depend on you to keep up an improved

lifestyle. You might need to realize what changes you bring with you.

## Real Estate Realities

Avoiding Common Pitfalls:

- Balance the allure of falling in love with a property from afar. Weigh it against the practicality of renting. It's easier to walk away from a rental.
- Consider the risks of buying land and building a house in another country.
- Unnoticed Restrictive Covenants or URCs:
- You've replaced the propane tanks, cut the grass, and trimmed the trees. But you failed to negotiate access to your property with your neighbor.
- The water situation can be hit-or-miss at times throughout the year. Having tanks might not be the fix you need. Conflicts over water overuse by newcomers are increasing.
- You have unknowingly encroached on the neighbor's land with your construction. You went beyond the property line.
- Dust or Mud. Which season do you prefer? Choose your home location wisely. Can you live with dust from a dry summer dirt road or mud in the rainy season?
- Are dogs barking in the neighborhood all night? You didn't see the place the night before you moved in. You were only there during the day when it was quiet.

## Buying a Problem

Here is a cautionary tale. The sales pitch reeled them in for a dreamy future. The place was paradise. It got them all excited about a dream they might never actually live. On the couple's fourth day, they bought a house. Retirement was far away, and moving wasn't in the plan. Are you renting it out? That slipped their minds. Also, they needed to speak Spanish. And they needed more local connections, which added to their challenges.

## Complicated Building Projects

You now live in a *New Culture,* and they practice *Conflict Avoidance.* You noticed a trend of workers arriving late and leaving early or the construction workers needing to return. Quality differences, legal problems, and selling an unfinished project can take time and effort. Selling a failed dream is like, well, a tough sell.

## Right of Possession

Wake up and smell the coffee! You are *A Stranger in a Strange Land.* You bought a property. Now, someone at your door claims strange *Rites of Demon Possession.* You can't force them out. You can't move into what you paid for. If you talk s*** about them in public, they file to have you pay, and they can put you in prison for damaging their honor. What the h***? And *You can't buy Title Insurance in Panama.*

This upsetting occurrence is still common in Panama. I have seen it many times. And not only with foreigners but with Panamanians as well. This one small piece of reality increases the chance of costly delays. Buying real estate in this country exposes you to the risk. Right of Possession Claims are expensive, upsetting, and a waste of time and energy. These sorts of problems people run into here. I wish it were uncommon.

## Creating an Escape Plan

Practical Considerations:

- Big investments like real estate, vehicles, and furniture require serious thought. It's a good idea to approach them cautiously or avoid them altogether.
- In Boquete, it is easy to buy and hard to sell.
- Plan a well-thought-out exit. Make it in case retirement in Boquete falls short.

- Avoid the Goofball Moves of the Arrogant. "No, you will not show them how it's done."

## Running From Your Problems

Don't lie to yourself. You can't solve issues with being overweight and language barriers by simply moving. You must face health concerns. Your well-being may be declining. Do you battle depression and anxiety? Are you withdrawing from society? Don't deceive yourself about your health. Also, don't lie to yourself about your relationships. Don't fool yourself about your finances. Acknowledge the work you need to do, to learn Spanish.

## Going Broke Buying Love

You meet someone online, fall in love despite a language barrier, and do it without meeting face to face. You invest in a fantasy, enchanted by it. You spend too much. It not only breaks your heart but also strains your finances. You start making sacrifices for the other to help them achieve their dreams.

There are extreme cases. The guy who sent an engagement ring to a woman? He started building a house with her before they were in the same room. They'd only chatted via video calls. Any guesses on who's name was on the title? It breaks my heart to think of all the similar situations.

## How To Avoid Snakes and Scorpions

I met an expat lady plumber a few years ago. She had a very odd pair of shoes on. One was a standard tennis shoe, and the other was a foam sandal shoe. I asked her what the deal was. She said, "I know I should be banging out my boots and shoes every time I put them on, but I didn't this time and got bit by a scorpion last week." She is right. Don't forget to bang out your shoes, sandals, or boots every time you put them on!

I learned this trick to avoid snakes from Panamanians. When you enter a bathroom, look around and check behind the toilet. Snakes are drawn to warm places when it gets cold in the afternoon and evening, so stay alert.

# Chapter 21
# Service, Volunteering, and Gratitude

I really love you guys. I call you my *super-fans.* I love the way you make me feel. I love to trade stories. You get me to tell you of long-forgotten things I've learned, seen, or done. You're the ones who make me dust off long-gone memories of places I've been. This story will guide you toward happiness in Boquete.

Once, when I was helping my mom run Meals on Wheels back in Ponca City, Oklahoma, we delivered free meals to the homebound, both handicapped and elderly. My mom gave me a big black trash bag and food for an old lady.

I asked, "Mama, what's this for?" She said, "This lady never throws anything away. We must steal back the old food and throw it out because she won't do it! She eats like a bird. And I've noticed since we started delivering here that she keeps pecking at the old stuff, and I think it will kill her."

My eyes bugged open, and I asked, "We're stealing her old food?" She answered, "Yep! And I need you to help me do it. I'm going to distract her in her back room. Before then, I'll stack up all the old stuff, so you grab it when she's not looking!" I was worried.

She said, "Head straight to the car and don't return. Hide it in the trunk where she can't see it. She will have a fit if she catches us, so we both have to be real careful about this, OK?" I nodded, shocked but in agreement, and we headed in.

Sure enough, her refrigerator was full of a library of crushed-down, half-food-filled clamshells from past deliveries. She whispered, "The other drivers don't do this, but they should. I'm sure it's because she has a hissy fit over it." She was a pack rat! My mama was right. She could die from this!

Hell! I could see from the stuff growing out of the ones on the bottom that she could be developing a deadly botulism strain. My mom beat on the door but then walked right in. It wasn't even locked. The old lady came, and my mom hugged and kissed her. Mom asked how she was doing and told her she loved her. She did it while diving into the refrigerator and pointing at the problem.

I thought, holy crap! She wasn't kidding. In a high, happy voice, she says to the lady, "Let's move some stuff around and make room for the new, OK?" Then she proceeds to stack the old stuff on a stool she's drugged out from the corner. Holy smokes, I thought! It was such a tall stack that it could not fit on the stool. She was stacking it on the floor, too.

Then my mom distracted her by pointing to pictures of the lady's family and asking her about them, and they wandered into the back. I stood there dumbfounded, horrified. Behind her back, mama pointed at me, wiggled her finger, and suddenly turned around and gave me a look a cat burglar would provide his partner when they see the owners stirring in their bed at night. She whispered, "Now!" I whipped out the bag hidden in my pocket, filled it up as quietly as possible, dashed for the door, and loaded it into the trunk. Then I hid, waiting in the car.

About three minutes later, my mama came out of that house with an enormous, satisfied grin and a happy gate. She gets back in and drives us to the next customer. And you know what she says to me with a big dumb grin? She says, *Those who Help are Happy! If we can, we should. Not for them. We do it for us. Your dad and I get such joy from doing this. You can't imagine.*

Boquete has a long list of volunteer opportunities. Volunteering is a good lifestyle choice here. It gets you out of the house, you will meet nice people, and you will serve the mission of the group you volunteer for. It's good for your heart; you'll feel great helping others.

Ride *The Joy Bus of Gratitude*. People who lead lives of service tend to be the happiest people ever. So I hope, happily, that you found this book to be of good service on your life journey.

# Chapter 22
# Boquete's Nicknames

## The Boquete Blue Zone

We are in a region known for its long life and health, which has attracted much attention from newcomers. People know Boquete, Panama, as a Blue Zone. It's widely recognized and celebrated for its exceptional qualities. My first hotel employee, *Belgica*, had four elders over 100 years old when we started!

Don Plinio would ask me to drive him to her house to see the *Elders*! That was funny because he was in his '90s. I would have coffee while he would wrestle with their big-toothed dog. He was quite the entertainer, making us all laugh. Boquete rejuvenates our senses, clears our minds, and restores a sense of calmness. It is excellent for the mind, body, and soul. It quickly improves the state of new humans after arrival. You start living like someone from a Blue Zone. You are almost forced to transition to a healthier and happier existence.

Boquete's blue zone effect owes much to the great socializing opportunities. We've got a pretty awesome *Coffee Shop Society*. It's effortless to meet and converse with someone in this town. If you don't want to be alone here, you don't have to be. The locals are super friendly, and newcomers and long-time residents mingle. You won't believe it, but you can socialize here no matter your language! People worldwide come to Boquete to soak up its one-of-a-kind lifestyle. They're drawn by its diverse cultural heritage and jaw-dropping natural beauty.

## The Bordeaux of Coffee

This is one well-earned nickname. We are blessed with the world's best coffee and the highest coffee prices (recently >$7,000/pound!). Our coffee dominates all others with rich and sophisticated flavors.

The world's coffee experts celebrate it for its smooth and velvety texture.

This coffee is a true indulgence for the senses. It produces the best, like the distinguished wine region it shares its name with. Encounter exquisite aromas and delicate caramel, chocolate, earth, and fruit notes. It makes it the perfect pick for coffee connoisseurs. They seek a luxurious and refined experience.

# The Perpetual Spring Valley

This Valley's constant or perpetual spring is well-known! The worst day here is about the same as Montana's best day of the year! Lol! I wake up at Zero Dark Thirty, head to the park after coffee, and stomp around in the jungle. It's springtime here, people! Yes! I'm talking about almost every day here. Rain and wind? That drives some people off. If you don't like perfection, don't come here. Keep your snow shovels. Our weather might only be for some. This garden of Eden might not be for you.

# The Fountain of Youth

Some consider Boquete to be the *Fountain of Youth*. We have hot springs nearby. But this nickname implies more than a legendary curative dip in magic waters! There is something in the water in Boquete! I know too many 80 and 90-year-olds who like to climb steep hills in the mountains so they can keep swinging a Machete!

The Indigenous Kings (Known as *Caciques*) have chosen this Valley for centuries. This is where they had their family farms. We have the burial grounds and petroglyphs to prove it. Here, they discovered their complex water diversion projects. This valley is an oasis. This area has the fabled *Blue Hole!* That is right. The valley's west side is often the only area with blue sky! Boquete is a timeless destination. People become more like their younger selves. That effect is more than only mystical allure.

# The Valley of Rainbows

This valley produces a great deal of Rainbows. Exotic orchids grow on the electric service wires! You must get frequent mist for this to happen, and we do. That and sunlight make up the rainbow powerhouse that is Boquete. We get rainbows in the morning and the afternoons. This area is unique for its incredible concentration of rainbows! Every time it rains, you may experience her magic. It's due to the sunshine mist that locals nicknamed *Bajareque!*

# The Disneyland of Panama

I made that one up. I am still jealous of my cousin Steve's record of sequential visits to Disneyland growing up. I am in my twelfth year here, rarely departing, so I may have him beat. I worked as the Concierge at my hotel, Hotel Central Boquete. I often had to explain why we had such a ridiculously long list of things to do here. I used the metaphor of Boquete as the "Disneyland of Panama." I wanted to help them understand why I had about 200 different options for activities. Things that were super fun, both free and paid to offer them! It blows their minds. "Oh! We should have planned for more days here in Boquete! We didn't know how great it was here!"

Chapter 23

# Why Do Retired Expats Move Home?

## To be Closer to Family

I talk to my sister almost every day. That works for us. We're very close. I also have two buddies back in the US. I speak with them every two or three days as well. I don't have biological children or grandchildren. Family is the number one reason expats go home.

It is more challenging for women. They need their grandbabies in their arms, while the husbands want to go hiking and fishing. This is a cause of many separations and divorces. If you're in a relationship, you need to work this issue out—and you need to do it before you make a move.

**Pro Tip:** "Know Thyself" is inscribed on the Temple of Apollo. It is the most famous of the Delphic Maxims, general rules from ancient Greece used to regulate behavior and thought.

Know your limits! I'm not simply talking about your abilities or your place in society. I'm also talking about the fact that you are a mortal being and will one day die. "To know thyself is the beginning of wisdom."– Socrates.

How do you deal with isolation and loneliness? Telephone therapy. We have modern tools, so you can see your loved ones while speaking to them. But I can't hug my sister on a video call. You must know your limits when living far from family and friends. And know your limits to change.

## Better Healthcare System Back Home

Navigating a foreign healthcare system is challenging. It's complicated here. That's why people pay to see a private Doctor who is bilingual. It's no problem if you've got the money. But what happens if you have a big problem? You must dive in and think about what can happen.

I want you to reframe the big question. I got good advice once from a chairman/chief of a tribe I work for up north. "Ain't nobody getting out of here alive. So, get going! Live while you're living." Now, I want you to ride with that one for a while. Put this book down. Sit on your porch or go for a walk. Yes, I'm talking about your mortality racing towards you. If you haven't done it before, this is an excellent time to think about everything.

Welcome back. I got another *zinger* for you. That first one dances along with the next one. It is Buddha's first great truth. "Life is suffering." I'm not selling gloom and doom. An attitude of gratitude will take the sting out. It's the only thing that can beat up fear and anger. I noticed that Panama deals with illness and death quite differently.

## The Problem of Over Treatment

My mom and dad had the deluxe Lutheran preacher package. It had endless insurance money to feed the system. And the system ran for profit. That's a cold-hearted thing. Mama got chased and finally tackled. Something called multiple myeloma took her down. I don't know what to call it, blood cancer, bone cancer, but it was a hell of a rough ride.

## Treat You to Death

She went in and out of remission so many times I lost count. They kept inventing new treatments. She never lost hope. They never stopped taking their insurance money. My mama never stopped fighting. And that's what they were selling her. Hope. She was like a great big oak tree they kept whittling on until all that was left was a toothpick. Misery is optional. Only you can choose to stop treatment.

In Panama, you won't get such a hard sales pitch. They talk about reality. Medical doctors here are different. They are a lot more honest. They are humane humans. They don't seem into it for the money. It freaks newcomers out. Medical Doctors give you their cell number and call to check on you every week. And house calls? Holy Crap! Yep, they still do that here.

You need to consider Medicare, Medicare Advantage, and private insurance for Panama. I'm not a Medicare expert but face these questions this year. There's a good chance they will start accepting Medicare here in Panama. I've heard the rumors for years, but now they might be true. I've already reviewed many ways Panama cares for you with public health. That is one of the unspoken giant benefits of residency here.

## Treatments Worse than Death

What if you get cancer? What if you get a severe heart problem? What if you have a complex health issue you've been managing for years, and it gets worse? That's a lot of what-ifs. Consider your options before the crisis. No one dies of old age. Something big comes up, and you might find better healthcare and support back home. And you leave.

I know people who have had hip and knee replacements in Panama. I know a guy who paid about $6,500 for an open heart surgery. He paid it out of his pocket. If you've read this far, you know I've got a severe heart condition. I accept the added risks of living in another country. I know myself. I've calculated the risks. I understand how Panama living protects and supports my health. It's a trade-off I agreed to years ago.

Chapter 24

# What Drives Newcomers Crazy

## Forewarned is Forearmed

Here's your basket full of stuff that seems to drive newcomers crazy. Look it up on the internet. Arturo and I had a vlog. "The Boquete Life Vlog" was its name. We did one called "Happy Chickens and Hungry Dogs!" You don't need an alarm clock anymore!

Around four in the morning, the roosters start crowing. They wake up the hungry dogs, and they start barking. You ask, "How can they live this way?" That is a lot of Booyah hours before dawn! Booyah means a happy ruckus. And that's when it starts happening. Their loyalty to the dream fails. Panamá Loco starts wearing off.

I have another story about roosters, which will violate my oath. In the last few years, I swore to no longer do five things. They're the five things that seem to set people off—hot-button issues. It looks like there's no benefit in talking about them. I want to be a businessman like Don Plinio. There's no need to make enemies. So here it is.

The first three: No more talking about politics, pandemics, or religion. The following two are more challenging. No more complaining or gossiping. I've explained this dozens of times, so folks around here know what is up. I look and point off in the distance and say, "Lookee there! Rainbows! Butterflies! And Unicorns!" I'm reminding them about my oath. I'm not wantin' to say anymore.

Hang on tight! This next piece is going to be a rough ride. And I'm violating my oath because I'm trying to give you an important lesson. What did the rooster crowing mean in the Bible? If you can get the message from this one, you might be able to ride this horse. *"Just because you can, doesn't mean you should. Ride better horses!"* I wrote that saying and have used it hundreds of times.

Hey kids! It looks like the Cowboy is doing the children's sermon this morning! So y'all are invited to bring your Mommies and Daddies with you if you wish. We're all going to sit in a big circle on our butts. Come up here in front of the altar. He's going to tell us a story about chickens.

"Way back when there was a man named Simon Peter. He was a famous guy. He hated chickens. It seems he got all torn up inside one day when he heard the first rooster crow. One of his best buddies had warned him. Before three roosters crowed in the morning, he would deny being friends with him. He would lie and say he didn't even know him.

When that cock crowed, it triggered terrible feelings about his failure of loyalty to his pal. Gentle Jesus! But his friend never gave up on him. He was that kind of guy."

So, what the hell am I talking about? I'm talking about *Panamá Loco*. I've seen it many times. It looks like a spiritual conversion. Folks become *True Believers*. They *know* Panama will save them.

And then the first cock crows, my lord almighty, at 3:30 a.m.! Then, the dogs start barking. And they begin to lose faith in the dream. Loyalty is constantly tested, like that guy called Simon Peter. When the rooster crows out your window, and you wake in the middle of the night pissed off. Remember my story. And go by my hotel and buy some of our fancy-ass gentle foam earplugs from 3M. You're going to need them.

So, keep the faith. Or put the coffee on. You can start getting up and going to bed with the *Gallinas de Patio or Backyard Chickens*. This will be one of your tests. Let me tell you about a few others.

## Mañana!

Down here, it doesn't mean tomorrow. It simply means not today. Panamanians do not like to fight. They are conflict avoiders. They have a problem saying no. Clear out the confusion. Yes and no can mean no. And tomorrow doesn't necessarily mean tomorrow. It only means not today. That is a *cultural* thing. You won't get them to change. It's how it is. It's the way they are.

When you move here, it's an *immersion program to learn patience!* We'll get you some if you need more patience when you get here. I'm talking about endurance, tolerance, self-restraint, and resignation. Patience is the ability to wait calmly for a long time without becoming upset. There is a shortage of that outside of Panama. And a glut of impatience. Expats seem to import it with them. Then, they try to spread it around. They think there's a shortage.

*Tranquilo.* That means *Don't Worry.* Take a chill pill. Set your watch to *Panama Time.* It looks like the good old U.S. here, but it is not. Panama has a Latin culture mixed with a secret sauce.

Recent genetic studies show 83% of Panamanians have Native American mitochondrial DNA. Back on the Rez, they used to say something that is now considered *politically incorrect.* The wrong words are *Indian Time.* I worked as a dentist for Indian Health Service Hospitals and Clinics. Tribal members would say, "What time should we show up? Are we starting on *Indian Time* or *White Man Time?*" No kidding!

# Happy Trails!

Let me use the attorney's term once again: *Attractive Hazard.* It's spectacular here. The beauty will hypnotize you. You won't be looking where you're driving or walking. Don't be a goofball. Stop moving, then go gawking around. I'm not kidding. It's a big problem.

It's like *Walking a Tightrope while Looking through a Kaleidoscope.* There's a good chance you're going to get bucked off. I have seen the damage: bloody arms and flat tires—or worse, lots worse.

Our great mayor (the famous mustache model) has built many new sidewalks and filled in untold numbers of potholes. But the holes and trip hazards are never-ending, some the size of foxholes. I try to avoid driving and walking in the dark. I run big tires and wear good boots when I have to. And I carry a small flashlight!

Remember, this is a rainforest, so road repairs may not last six months. The engineers say it's hydrostatic pressure or something. The water can lift the patch right out. It is not the most stable place to live on a volcano. Not *Tierra Firme* or *Firm Land*.

**ProTip:** See where you're going at night! Buy a *Strong LED Mini-Flashlight and Clip it to your Keychain.*

Here's a *punny* joke. The word *Boquete* can also be translated as *Hole*. But *Hueco* is the most common word for *Hole*. *Huecoron* is slang for *Holes Everywhere*. You might say, *"Boquete es un Huecoron!"* That translates to *Boquete, which is a hole covered in holes*. Lol!

## Clean as a Whistle!

I hear you need to move to Colombia if you're looking for that. They say it's spotless. Here you better take care; don't step in dog poop. They don't always pick up after their hounds. Or themselves. The trash can be bad, especially after parades. I've seen busloads of people throwing all their trash out the windows on the way out of town! It drives us crazy.

The mayor has lots of people running around picking up after everybody. And so do some foreigners in that Basura Busters group I told you about. It gets ridiculous after parades, festivals, and holidays. Notice that the whole neighborhood comes out with trash bags early in the morning after. They pick up after the visitors leave.

Chapter 25
# Modern Conveniences

## The Air Conditioning Question

I've lost count of how many times guests have walked into their room at my B&B and freaked out. This is due to the lack of air conditioning; we only have fans. It's always the same reaction: "Where's the AC? I can't survive without it! It's too hot in here! How can you run a hotel without AC?!"

My responses vary depending on how I feel and how much I've slept. It could be like, "Hey, this is like the garden of Eden - no need for AC or heating here, ma'am!" Or "Nobody here bothers with air conditioning or heating! Windows are wide open 24/7! Take a drive around and see all those doors swinging open! We skip it because we don't need it. And the biting bugs here aren't that bad."

## Temperature changes with elevation

Hey, a heads up! If you climb 1000 feet up the mountain, it'll be around 4°F cooler. And if you live 1000 feet below the village, you can expect it to be about 4° warmer. That is a simple trick to figure out your ideal climate here. If you like the southern Florida climate, visit the nearby Potrerillos village. It has an *Arriba and Abajo (Upper and Lower)* section. It's only 13 km or 8 miles away.

You can cruise through *Palmira.* Then, hop on the new roller coaster-like road to Potrerillos Arriba. It is 7.1 km or 4 1/2 miles away. The climate there is slightly cooler than below but still warmer than in Boquete. Fun fact - we've got a few "Arribas" and "Abajos" right here in Boquete too!

## 150 Distinct Microclimates.

Seneca was a renowned philosopher. He once said, "If a man doesn't know his destination, no wind is favorable." These microclimates pack a lot into small spaces. When I strolled to my hotel, I would transition from rainbows and sunshine to a sudden rainstorm and back.

Our Rotary Club renovated the small park, which now has a playground and a half-court soccer field for the kids. People call it *The M&M Park* because the round rocks of the Levee were painted in those colors. Its actual name is *Parque El Tropezón Infantil*. The direct translation is *Children's Stumble Park!* But they mean it is the kid zone. Many neighbors volunteered to assist in its reconstruction.

One volunteer, a foreigner, had been residing across the street with his girlfriend. One day, he walked past me in front of my hotel. I am wielding a machete, trimming the bushes. He reported that he had split from his girlfriend. He had moved to a cheap place eastward, across the valley. "Nestled in the mountains of *'Jaramillo Arriba.'*"

He told me, "Tim, it's got a breathtaking view. It sits atop a cliff. It is behind a grand house. Intended for the gardener, it rents for a mere $350 per month. It includes everything, including utilities, internet, and cable."

He explained. "Small problem with the place. I was unaware of the peculiar climate they have up there! It's such a cloud forest. Clouds come right in my cabin. It is not like the park down below. There, it is a completely different climate. It's so humid! It is like breathing vapor from a steamer or old-fashioned humidifier."

The following few details surprised me. "If I leave a door or window ajar, my TV screen picks up condensation! I have to keep wiping it off! And my leather boots are sprouting flowers! Each night, everything turns damp. I have to seal it up and run two dehumidifiers. Every morning, both are full. I kind of miss my old girlfriend and her place. It's like being in a completely different world up there."

# Dishwashers, Disposals, Trash Compactors, and Dryers

I wonder if many homes have all four of those items. Realtors are telling me odd stories. They say that newcomers, especially women, walk out when they see a home they are being shown that do not have them. "No dishwasher or dryer! No way!"

Dishwashers are super rare here. I have never loaded one in this country, and I know they sell them. I'm sure I'm not the only one who's noticed this phenomenon. Some developers have thought about these wants. They're including them in the new housing units popping up in our valley.

This everyday disposal item in your kitchen sink is uncommon here. There are frequent plumbing problems in Panama, which adds a lot of stress to your home system. I live in a little cabin next to a creek. Instead of a disposal, I have a little compost pile outside my window by the creek my landlord and I toss into. It seems to work out fine, especially for the White Rabbit who feeds there morning and evening!

I've never seen a trash compactor in anyone's home here in Panama. I suppose they have to be here somewhere, but where? It is one more reason why rental and sale properties are rejected.

In our community, dryers are a luxury item. Almost everybody has a clothesline and uses them. This can cause some trouble during the more challenging parts of the rainy season. I have had my clothes rained on many times because I got home a little too late. Sometimes, I put them on hangers to run out and grab them when the rain starts.

When I needed something washed and dried quickly and had no time to look for a dryer, I turned to my dehumidifier. During the rainy season, the humidity is high. Water condenses and runs down your walls and windows when it cools at night. That can cause mold and mildew, which is dangerous for your health.

I have a good, small clothes washer. When it's done, my clothes are very, very dry. If it looks like rain, I put everything on hangers in the bathroom with my dehumidifier and the door open. If I bring stuff almost dry from the clothesline, I point my pedestal fan at it for a few hours. That's good enough.

Chapter 26
# Hiring Help

## Panama's Employment and Labor Laws

What about Hiring a ½ Day/Week Maid?

In Panama, labor laws state that a day shift employee should work a maximum of 8 hours per day and 48 hours per week.
Part-time workers such as housekeepers or maids should ensure their working hours stay within these limits to avoid the necessity of a formal employment contract. But I am not an Attorney. Get legal advice.

To maintain compliance and avoid issues, it is advisable to:

- Ensure compliance with legal working hour limits.
- For any part-time role, it's advisable to establish a written agreement detailing responsibilities, work hours, and compensation. This can help safeguard both yourself and the housekeeper.
- Consider the necessity of social security contributions, as all earnings are liable to income taxes, social security levies, and contributions to an education fund.
- This should not present any problems for up to half a day each week, provided the total hours do not surpass the legal daily and weekly limits.
- *Consulting with a local labor law expert or attorney is advisable to ensure complete adherence to Panamanian labor laws.*

Minimum Age for Employment in Panama:

- In Panama, the legal working age is 18.
- Children under 14 are prohibited from employment.
- Those aged 15 without a primary education are not eligible.

- Individuals between 14 and 17 should avoid hazardous industries that involve alcohol, electricity, transportation, flammable materials, or underground tasks.
- Night shifts, work on public holidays, and weekends are not permitted.

Guidelines on Bonus and 13th Month Pay in Panama:

- Employees receive an additional month's salary as a thirteen-month bonus, paid in three equal parts in April, August, and December.
- Day shift employees work a maximum of 8 hours daily, while night shift workers have a 7-hour limit.
- The weekly maximum for day shifts is 48 hours, with most employees working a 44-hour week.

Fixed Term and Contract Employees:

In Panama, employers are required to furnish written employment agreements for their workers in compliance with labor regulations. These contracts may be fixed-term or indefinite and tailored to various job categories. While Spanish is the primary language for agreements, English is also frequently utilized.
Panamanian labor law sets the minimum wages based on occupation, business size, and activity, ranging from USD 326.56 to USD 971.35 monthly. Employers must also give a 13th-month pay, equal to an extra month's salary, paid in April, August, and December.

# Working Hours and Overtime Pay

According to labor law, the typical working hours for a full-time employee in Panama are 8 hours a day spread over a six-day workweek (totaling 48 hours a month). However, workers aged fourteen to seventeen are limited to a 36-hour workweek.
In Panama, the typical work week spans from Monday through Friday.

155

An employee who works beyond regular hours is eligible for overtime compensation. This pay is governed by collective agreement, employment contract, or Panamanian labor laws. The maximum overtime a worker can log is three hours daily and nine hours weekly.

No overtime is allowed for hazardous work.

Overtime Pay Rate in Panama:

- Additional hours between 6:00 am and 6:00 pm are compensated at 125% of an employee's gross pay.
- Extra hours worked between 6:00 pm and 6:00 am, on a day off, or holidays are paid at 150% of the employee's gross pay.
- For employees working the night shift, any extra hours will be paid at 175% of their gross salary.

## Entitlement to Leave

Annual Leave - 30 days:

- The duration of annual leave depends on the length of employment, requiring a minimum tenure of 12 months.
- Employers must remit payment for these leaves at least three days before the leave commencement.
- Panamanian labor regulations mandate that employers in Panama must grant paid leave to their employees, known as statutory leaves.
- Full-time employees, by law, are entitled to paid annual leave.

Public Holidays - 11 days:

- All part-time and full-time staff members have the right to enjoy public holidays.

- Employees asked to work on public holidays must receive overtime pay.

Sick Leave - 18 days

- Full-time employees have the right to paid sick leave.
- Employers must compensate sick leave at 100% of the employee's gross salary.
- Employees must furnish a medical certificate from a registered practitioner to utilize sick leave benefits.

Maternity Leave - 14 weeks. Adoptive parents - 28 days.

Note: Full-time employees have the right to paid maternity leave.

- Maternity leaves kick in six weeks before the expected due date and wrap up eight weeks after delivery.
- Panamanian Social Security provides maternity pay. However, the employee must have made at least nine months' contributions to social security before reaching the ninth month of pregnancy.
- If the employee doesn't meet their contribution, the employer must cover the remaining amount, calculated based on the last or average salary over 180 days.
- Employees may prolong their leave entitlement with a certificate from a registered medical practitioner for complex deliveries or multiple births.

# Chapter 27

# Paid Public Holidays in Panama

## 2024

January 1 – *New Year's Day/Año Nuevo*

January 9 – *Martyrs' Day/Día de los Mártires* - Martyrs' Day in Panama commemorates the 1964 anti-American riots over the Panama Canal Zone's sovereignty. This event, also known as the Flag Incident, led to the U.S.'s decision to transfer Canal Zone control to Panama in 1977.

February 15-18 - *Carnival* - This is a four-day event, while the National Labor Holiday is only two days long. *Martes Carnival's* last day is crazy! There is no parade in Boquete, but it is a massive event in Las Tablas.

March/April - *Easter holidays - Good Friday and Holy Saturday* are *Viernes y Sábado Santos, Easter Sunday/Pascua,* or *Resurrection Sunday/Domingo de Resurrección.*

May 1 – *Labor Day/Día del Trabajador*

November 3 – *Colombia Independence Day/Independencia de Colombia*

November 4 – *Flag Day/Día de la Bandera*

November 5 – *Colón Province Separation Movement/Movimiento de Separación en Colón*

November 10 – *First Cry of Independence from Spain/Primer Grito de Independencia de España*

November 28 – *Panama's Independence Day/Independencia de Panamá* (from Spain)

December 8 – *Mother's Day/Día de la Madre*

December 25 – *Christmas Day/Navidad*

**Pro tip:** Familiarize yourself with the term *"Dia Feriado."* These are national public holidays in Panama, during which employees are to receive additional compensation per Panamanian labor laws. Working these days guarantees double pay, also known as "double time," aligning with Panama's labor laws that mandate increased compensation for employees working on statutory public holidays.

Panama observes multiple paid national holidays, including the day of a president's inauguration, also recognized as a paid holiday. Numerous other celebrations are considered national events, yet they may only sometimes feature on the official paid holiday calendar. On January 6, we celebrate *Día de los Reyes (Magi Day)*, and on August 15, we commemorate *Fundación de Panamá La Vieja (Foundation Day of Historical Panama)*.
November is a lively month filled with patriotic celebrations in Panama. It's known as *Mes de la Patria* or *Patriotic Month*. It's all about commemorating Panama's liberation from Spain and Colombia.
Remember: If a public holiday falls on a Sunday, it will be observed on Monday.

# Fines

Non-compliance with Panamanian labor laws incurs various penalties, including:

Employers who force their employees to surpass the stipulated overtime limit (9 hours per week) will be required to compensate 75% of their gross salary and pay an additional penalty.
In wrongful termination cases, employers must compensate employees for any outstanding payments amounting to $2,000.00 or more.

Chapter 28

# You Saved My Life!

## I met a Guy!

When I reminisce about meeting Guy, it reminds me of Gabriel García Márquez's novel Love in the Time of Cholera. The themes in our first coffee shop chat align closely with the novel. Like an epidemic, love can bring about physical afflictions like a plague. Whether in the book or Guy's reflections on our happenstance encounter, our stories illustrate that the true essence of love reveals itself only with time.

Without love, immense suffering wouldn't exist. The stories we shared show this is the price one willingly pays for its great value. My story begins at my hotel right after I finished my daily swimming at Valle Escondido. It was a warm, still evening, as dark was creeping into the Valley. I silently slid my tiny, white Suzuki Jimny 4x4, coasting, lights out, downhill to the drive-through coffee order window.

I stopped at the open order window to check on my receptionist/barista. She wasn't in sight, but I saw a man wearing a surgical mask sitting alone. He was a quiet man. He was sitting across the way, by the main entry, at a tall four-top table that barely had space for two. He was almost outside there, sitting in the double-door entry. Both of the ancient wooden glass doors were rarely opened. It was a lucky, warm evening without a breeze. He sat facing the last light.

He hadn't heard me approach. Perched in front of him sat one of our oversized, hot, heavy ceramic, white, 16-oz. Cappuccino coffee cups, saucer, and spoon. He was in-distractible, totally engrossed in the phone in his hand. He was alone with his thoughts, doom scrolling or something.

I did not see my receptionist/barista anywhere, so after a moment or two, I yodeled, *"Buenas!"* (a common greeting here that means

*Hello Good)* in an attempt to locate and check in with her. The guy on the far side looked over quickly. I studied me with difficulty through the glass sides of our pie and soda cooler. He stood to see over it and suddenly reacted with recognition. He took a step over and gave me another stare.

I see he is unsure. I've got a mask on, too—his head jets forward to see me better. Then, my receptionist approaches, peeking at me through the window. Quietly, I whisper to her, "Super Fan?" She slowly nods and church-whispers back, "Oh Yeah!"

Then, the fellow pops out of his chair and walks over to the cooler to better look at me. His eyes over his mask sparkle with recognition, and his ears rise and tighten his mask by his hidden grin. I say, loud enough for both of them to hear, "I'll park in the back. I will join you for a cup of coffee, Buddy."

In full protest, he says, "No, no, no, you don't have to do that!" He waves his hands in front of him to show me that it's unnecessary. I loved his strong accent. I said, "No problem! It gives me an excuse to come in for a late coffee and a friendly chat." I park my rig in the back and wander through the back-gardened terrace to the coffee shop.

On my way to his table, I see him standing, a bit excited. As I slide by Yari, I order up my favorite combo. "How about a 12-ounce Americano, two teaspoons of the *Dorado (raw, whole sugar-cane sugar)*, and a *Holly Dolly* dessert bar (Panamanian slang for the chocolate and coconut bar known as a *Hello Dolly!*)."

He gestures to offer me his chair as he moves his coffee to the other side, next to a small pile of travel fluff. This gracious action makes me feel welcomed and relaxed. I'm the kind of cowboy who has long enjoyed the comforts of keeping his back to the wall.

I sit down, and we introduce ourselves. The man in the coffee shop is "Guy" or "Gee" in French. I tell him my name is "Tim" or "Timoteo" in Spanish. His accent was terrific.

While punctuating excitedly in the air with his hands, he explains, "I know who you are. I've seen all your videos on da YouTube, some of dem over and over again a bunches of times." I say, "Oh, thank you kindly. I was curious and asked Guy, "So, what did you think of my videos?"

He sat quietly, looking at me over his mask for a long moment. I couldn't read him. He looked like he was struggling for an answer. After a long moment, he blurted out, "*Joo Save My Life!* Jor na gonna believe dis, but I feel like I know joo already. Doz walking and talking videos of Jors! You can imagine what diz mean to me!"

Frankly, I've heard lovely feedback on my YouTube videos many times. But what he'd said about saving his life stopped me in my tracks. We sat for a moment of silence, staring at each other. He leans towards me and spits it out again, even more full of heart and emotion. "Joo Save My Life!"

I was stunned. I asked, "what do you mean?" He repeated it a third time. "Joo save my life! Joo understan me now? Joo Did! Joo really did it! It was joo." "I know I just met joo, but I feel like I already know joo, like a friend. For once, I was speechless.

"Look a Joo! Joo are just like joo self, on doz videos." He struggled to find the right words in English. "Joo were like a lifeline, tossed out due me, like a man lost at sea. Let me tell joo why and how dis happen. Joo, why I'm here today." I settled back in my chair as he continued with his story.

"Dee first six months after my wife died... it was bad, real bad. I could na do no-tin. I wasn't taking care of myself. My son, her son, actually my stepson, but he's my son. You know. He got da real worried bout me, kept coming over talking and talking, me only sitting, never doing no-ting, he was getting kind of scared-like, over me.

And he was right da worry. I jus din want to live no more. I was alone." I said, "That's too bad." He said, "It was in dat next year, after dat, I started tinkin'. Like, bout what dee boy tole me over and over. Eyes really do got to do something with my life. I yoost can't sit here locked up in dis house alone, not living, not doing nah-tin, no plan forever!

162

Joo sees, Tim, I never took no help. I did every-ting for her. I put a little ting next dooer bed so in case she wakes up scared or hurding in da night I would be dare for her, to calm her, to help her, you see?" He paused, lost in the memory. Then he stormed out with, "Tim, she fought! We fought dem damn problems of hers! We fought it for two long years together."

He paused and started again. "I quit my damn job so I could stay home by her side. I din care about no-tin else. Day said I should na do it!" He stopped to catch his breath and wipe tears, then said, "Tim! It was jus so terrible! I woon-na let no one help me! I got mad, kinda crazy, yelled at dem guys, dem government sent helpers. I chased dem away. I had to do it all for her! "

I was da one. Tim, joo can no a-mah-jin!" But I did. I was. A story my mom told and made me promise not to forget. A tale long gone away. Behind my mask, he could see I was crying too, remembering how my Dad had cared for Mom night and day, not a complaint, to the best of his ability, even after he had a severe stroke.

He didn't know my mama fought cancer. There were so many new treatments and periods of remission, but it always came back. She never quit fighting, and she never lost hope. That was after my dad had his little stroke, but he'd learned to talk and walk again.

The story's themes told by the man in the coffee shop are the same as those in the novel. Lovesickness can be like a plague and can cause physical illness. The stories told in that novel and by the man sitting, drinking coffee, and wondering if he will meet me show that it's only over time that we can understand how valuable love is.

So, in the end, this book you're reading is really a love story. It's about the people drawn toward this tropical world and into my life. Because of the hotel I built and the YouTube videos I created they found along their way, looking to start over in *Paradise*.

Guy says I saved his life, but he's the one who's been living a great come-back story in Boquete. Guy fell from the heavens and landed standing. (*Se Cayó del Cielo Parado*). Fast-forward: He and Iris, my friend and favorite Calzone maker at her famous *Riccos Pizzeria* restaurants, are building apartments, a home, and a new restaurant at the booming police stop area! It is located on the Boquete side of the checkpoint, on the west side of the road, a short way away.

So, pick up some inspiration and pizza on your way to Boquete! And please support *The Best Calzone in the World.* (+507-6570-0517 - Riccos Pizzeria) They are stuffed with love and wonder! Double down on her secret sauce.

And Guy, thank you for allowing me to share your inspiring come-back story.

# Chapter 29
# The Life Unlived

## Your Old Story

I'm guessing I'm onto something here. It's no coincidence you've made it this far or that you're deep in this book! Is life as you know it, your everyday world, starting to look like an old black-and-white movie? Let's take a look at *Your Old Story*. There are likely some positives and negatives. The same show keeps playing, which makes it all too cozy.

Are you feeling the urge for a new adventure? Have you started crafting a fresh story in your mind? It sounds a bit wild. Are you feeling hesitant about it? Are you sharing your plans with loved ones or friends? When they try cooling you off with a "Hey, listen," chill-out vibe, you know it's time to hit the road. What do you think? *You are thinking.* That is what is essential.

## Facing the Threshold

I'm sure you've received some, let's say, "reluctant" feedback. You're checking out the retirement abroad scene. You've seen countless videos of potential retirement spots. You see folks living it up in unique, beautiful places. You dream of joining them and making new friends.

Significant changes can be scary. The people in the videos felt this. Are you feeling freaked out?

**Pro Tip:** Try this easy breathing trick to relax. Do two fast, hard inhales through your nose. Then, do a slow exhale through pursed lips. Do it 3-4 times outside, eyeballs getting sunshine, gazing unfocused at the horizon. It is a tweak to your autonomic nervous system from Dr. Huberman.

Dr. Huberman's Podcast has excellent tips. It shows the public the latest in Brain and Eye Research. He interviews a diverse list of Experts. He also does research with a team he leads at Huberman Lab, Stanford University.

That's a triple Huberman habit stack: Breathing, Sun in your eyes, and staring unfocused. It's easy and effective! Meditation for the rushed. Try it out. It doesn't cost you anything.

Now, you see your old and new stories with a relaxed body and a focused mind. Oh my god! You have it dawn on you. I could do this, too. And I want to. This latest story is going to bring *Radical Change* to my life!

## Your New Life

What do you want? To find what you love. Why do you like it? *Reasons* come first. The *How* comes later. Now's the time to get serious about your dreams. Develop your vision. Discover your purpose. Find and face your truths. Be honest with where you're at and where you want to be. There will be no retakes. The show of your life is going live right now.

**Pro-Tip:** Check out the book, *"Ask and It is Given: Learning to Manifest Your Desires."* This is a self-help book about Manifestation and Law of Attraction book by Esther and Jerry Hicks.It delivers a simple formula for how to ask for and receive whatever you want to be, do, or have. What you are asking for is what you are being given.

## Get a Hungry Why

Build on that hunger. Create a bigger *Why*. That creates a smaller *How*. It's in your head. Work on yourself. Envision a life that makes you happy. A greater purpose may have called you. It's time to wake up. It's time to ask for what you want. Activate that hunger. Then, pick an identity as someone who gets what they want. See it in your mind. Your vision. Your dream. Who is your hero, or how could you be one?

Be careful what you are asking for, you might get it! *"Ask, and It is Given."* That's the secret, you know. It's no big deal, do a little rebirthing. Ask for the right thing. You can reform your identity. Start with the simple. And what you do becomes what you are.

Here is your example, me.

Tim is a film and writer guy.

Or spice it up. The new guy comes up and says, "You are Tim? The Film and Writer Guy, yes?" I say, "Yeah, that's me." He cuts to the chase and asks the best question of all. He says, "Why Tim? Why do you do it?"

I have embraced who I am. I have a long, exciting list of things I used to do. But I am doing something else now. I am now procrastinating on manuscript edits. I rebel. I create a bunch of new videos. I do a quick film edit and posting. Then I start writing about something else. That's my latest story. Creator Guy. I am a guy in the lucky land of Panama with a manuscript in hand, writing and filming away.

Here is a little test for you. Describe a random person nearby. Stop! Look at them now and describe them. Did you use something he did or does, or only what they look like? Do the inventory. Many used to be x,y,z, and fill-in-the-blank people. Are people prone to describe you by what you do or what you did?

If it is all *I did* and not *I do*, you need to get going. That is unless you traveled to the moon as an astronaut. Then you're done. So, let me summarize. Identity is like a quick summary of a person. It's like a mini CV (Curriculum Vitae or Resume). It changes over time because you are *doing it*. That makes you *become it*.

The trick is to identify the identity of the character you want to play and then take action along the way to being that person. I listened to Arnold Schwarzenegger's new Audiobook, "Be Useful: 7 Tools for Life." He was into his body-building heroes. His poor dad thought he was fruity or something. All the posters on his wall were muscle men all oiled up and flexing. He idolized them and wanted to become like them! He wanted to leave Austria and go to America.

Life changes us over time. It did in yours. It did in mine. Look back at life and see how it came. Was it like the weather at the seashore, the seasons passing by? Notice the Identity you held in each passage. We are different people at different stages of our lives. If we are lucky to have a long life, we can look back at the people we have been.

For some, retirement is more challenging than for others. That's why many keep a side hustle. You don't need the money, but it keeps you busy and out of trouble. I know a guy in town who runs a bar to stay active. It sure is more men than women who keep working. Retirement doesn't brutalize women. They ride it better.

Retirement, huh? It's a big deal. It feels almost like a demon possession for some. Imagine you're that little train car, and the boy decides it's time to retire you and takes you off the tracks. Sound familiar?

Here's some homework. Grab a piece of paper and fill out the next section with your answers. My story is your example/guide.

Then, extreme snowmobiling, ice spikes on my horse's shoes, training working cow dogs, Indian Reservations, and ceremonies.

My old story, Cowboy. Dentist, on many Indian Reservations. Cowboying for better places to ride, doing Dentistry for food and shelter.

The long past is about sailing, windsurfing, SCUBA diving, Mexico, and Central America.

Before that came maps, compass, backpacking, Appalachian Trail, and hitchhiking.

Before that, Little Timmy liked to ride Silver in the bullpens with his Grandpa Levi on the ranch.

# Rewrite Your Story

It is how we see ourselves and our stories about our lives—the ones we tell ourselves. Stories make up memories. They are powerful.

Stories can take you anywhere. In Boquete, I have seen people rewrite their stories and do incredible things. Fill in the blanks when you meet the people here.

The person needed something, and they did the holy smoke. And they have been to hell for who knows why. Now they are here, writing a new chapter to their life story. We find them every day on our streets. Like cream, they've risen to the top.

I have seen wild horses crossing far in the wilderness, a broad X cut into stone. Boquete is the same. The people who get here are like wild horses running across rivers of other wild horses. That is why life here is so rich and complex. The locals, foreigners, and newcomers all mix.

That all happens at the crossroads of the volcano, Boquete.

# How to Power Up

**Pro Tip:** There are two ways to play your mind and body like a banjo. Music and movement energize both.

*First One:* Use music to increase your energy and feel great. Feel powerful, get inspired, and enter a flow state.

Second One: Remember to raise energy and brain hormones and drop stress hormones. Jump out of bed and scream at the mirror in a power pose like Superman: "I'm moving to Panama!" Do it every day.

Check out the Tony Robbins videos about *power posing*. It is backed by science and puts you into a high-energy state, immediately improves your mood, and makes you more willing to take risks.

I am a superfan of the singer Mike Posner. His song "Keep Going" has a great line: "*I just want to live before I die.*" He had a list of what he wanted to do but was doing what he thought other people wanted him to do. Then his dad died, and a friend died, and another did.

Go down that rabbit hole. Mike is a musician with a great message. He discovered what he loved. His music will charge your batteries. Music is a trick to increase your energy. He's got some songs that will improve your state of being.

## Bucket List Time

On that list of Mike Posner's was, "I want to walk across America." Then, at mile 1800, a rattlesnake bit him. He nearly died, requiring transportation by helicopter. He was admitted to the hospital and had to learn how to walk again. Then he continued walking to the coast.

He says one of the biggest blessings was all the people he connected with on the way. He realized he would have never been able to do that without walking so far. A lot of people joined him walking. The vision was to walk America. The gift he got was a strong bond with people. They are the reason he makes music.

## I.D. the Barriers

You must first find it. Before you can face it, what is the truth? Where are you now? Where do you want to be? What stops you from getting from one to the other? Is it fear? Is it a habit? Do you need a set of skills?

Close the gap. Figure out how to overcome the barriers to success. Is it in your head? Is it psychological? Fears and phobias can act like corrections officers. Or is it with your hands and feet? The mechanics get in the way, And you take no action. Frustration builds.

## Draw your MAP

Decide what you want. Write down the list of things to do to get you there. That is your map. Jot down at the top the one simple thing you can do to get started. Mark Twain said, "The secret of getting ahead is getting started." Identify the first small thing you can do that would get you started.

Break the rest of it down into the tiniest little bits. That is going to be huge. It is your *Massive Action Plan* (MAP). Make your steps so small it's easy to feel successful. It will give you surges of dopamine that power your journey. *Underline* the 20% of the steps that get you 80% of the way there. See the power that 20% has in reaching your goal.

Put it in a document with check boxes next to it. Yes, every little step. Then, you won't start walking and get lost. You need to be able to measure and feel your progress on your MAP going forward. This is it. Look at it. What's your new story?

**Pro Tip:** Focus is a force multiplier on work.

"Almost everyone I've ever met would be well served by spending more time thinking about what to focus on. It is much more important to work on the right thing than it is to work for many hours. Most people waste most of their time on stuff that doesn't matter.

Once you have figured out what to do, become unstoppable about getting your small handful of priorities accomplished quickly. I have yet to meet a slow-moving person who is very successful."

-Sam Altman, CEO of OpenAI

# Do the Hard Thing First

For me, that was downsizing. I had a ridiculous amount of stuff. Stupid giant doctor home; it and my storage units were full of stuff. My Viking ancestors had a great saying for all this. "Own only what you can carry." That's a simple guide for minimalism, isn't it?

Have you heard about *Viking Hordes*? Some damn farmer in Norway pulls out a big stone from his field, then, what the heck! That hole is brim full of pillaged silver and gold! Imagine the wealth and instability of their world.

Do what you have to do to get free. *Take Massive Action.* My mama was a pack rat—or a librarian. She had boxes of mementos from every step of our lives filed in them. She had narrowed it down to only a hundred boxes in the last years of her life. She started to give the contents away. She felt it was too much to leave behind for us to deal with.

She gave me good advice on downsizing. She said, "Take a picture of it, hold it in your hands, and stare at it for a while, then sell it or give it away!" I sent five big trucks to my church back in Montana for their annual garage sale fundraiser. I got an enormous tax credit for my donation!

**Pro Tip:** Wander over to check out
https://www.languagetransfer.org/. That is another excellent way to learn Spanish online.

Start your Spanish classes today. Learning a language takes work. Take it like daily medicine. Learning a language prevents Alzheimer's! While drinking your first coffee of the day, spend 5-10 minutes learning Spanish. I bet after 5 minutes, you can't stop for half an hour. Hustle up and get going!

## Start Stacking Habits

Create a daily practice that supports you in chasing your dream. You know what you should be doing. When I first wake up, I do a funny exercise called Dr. Mercola's Nitric Oxide Release Workout. Find it at https://www.youtube.com/watch?v=qEui9ImJaiI. Then, I start drinking two cups of water. I do that exercise when writing to loosen up. In the middle of the morning, I meditate for 15 minutes. I'm like the Beatles. I try to do Transcendental Meditation, https://www.tm.org/en-us/, twice a day or twenty minutes of Non-Sleep Deep Rest (NSDR), https://youtu.be/hEypv90GzDE?si=9kzHoetJX9SnhTH9, daily.

I bought myself a beautiful business ledger book. In it, I write about what happened the day before, share my thoughts, and write about what I'm grateful for. Gratitude is the attitude that pays big bucks. It gives you energy and immediately improves your body's stress and energy hormones.

Then, listen to something inspiring. If I finish this book, I'll make an audiobook so you can hear it in the mornings while walking. Get outside and get some sunshine on your eyes. They say that's great for you as well. Lay your exercise outfit on a chair beside your bed before sleeping. Stack up some good habits. You know what little things you could be doing every day. This stack of habits will help you move forward.

## Raise Standards and Measure Success

Remember, you're trying to become your true self. At this stage, stop tolerating in yourself and others what you can't go along with in your new life. We get done what we measure. Chart it out in your Journal somehow. Are you acting depressed, anxious, or isolated? Did you wake up and see the sunshine? Did you go for a walk? How are you doing on downsizing?

Manage the creation of your new life by measuring it. If you don't stand for something, you'll stand for anything. It's time to up your game. It's time to make some goals. How will you score if you still need to know where the touchdown line is?

Celebrate the little victories along your way. Build on your success. Remember to give back. If you get off track, restart the process. If you stay on track, consider what you want. What are your next-level goals? Celebrate your Accomplishments. Keep going!

Remember my dad's last words, *"You can do it!"*

# Chapter 30
# **Conclusion**

Are you ready? Boquete, Panama, is an excellent spot for expats, retirees, and digital nomads. Come check out our Coffee and Flowers. Visit our sparkling seas. Walk the tranquil streets. Choose a budget-friendly life tucked away in the hills, retired in Boquete, Panama.

As we conclude this guide, I want to share a simple three-step process that will take you from dreaming about a great retirement to living one.

## **Step 1: Inventory - Using the Franklin T-Test**

An honest self-assessment is crucial during the critical inventory phase.

Take the famous Ben Franklin T-Test. Build a pros and cons list with specifics.

Assess your pluses and minuses of moving to Boquete. Create your personalized decision-making guide.

Draw a line down the center of a piece of paper. Add a plus sign (+) top left and a minus sign (-) top right.

Going down the left side, list your reasons for retiring to Boquete. Think temperate climate, lower cost of living, and welcoming expat community. But what appeals to you?

On the right, jot down potential drawbacks or things holding you back. These include being far from family. The struggle of learning a new language is also a challenge. And feeling hesitant about leaving the familiar is hard, too.

**Pro Tip:** Here's a helpful quote from the book "Lightning Strike" by William Kent Krueger:

*"One thing I know, if something scares you, the best thing to do is take action. Give yourself a sense that you have a measure of control."*

You will make balanced decisions when you organize your thoughts on both sides of the ledger. Let it rip. Please write it down. Then, take action on what scares you.

Let your heart speak. Let your mind be wise as well. Consider all factors.

## Step 2: Decision - Ponder Your Path

What do you do now? What steps must you take? The picture should be clearer post-inventory. Visions of the gentle murmur of Boquete's rivers and the draw of an affordable utopia may sway your heart. Then, you will tilt towards taking a brave step forward.

A positive balance sheet only sometimes calls for quick action. Your decision may also involve setting a timeline. You can gather more information by visiting Boquete.

Consider where you live, money, health care needs, and love for adventure.

Retiring in paradise is not a lifestyle choice—it's an enormous life decision. You must consider the legal and logistical steps to lay the groundwork for a smooth transition, which is necessary for moving to Panama.

## Step 3: Action - Next Steps Made Clear

Make the call. Embrace Your Path to Progress.It's time to take the actions outlined in my free ebook. It guides you from decision to action.

Action Step: Did you visit the following link to get access to my Free Ebook?

*"How To Retire In Paradise In As Little As 4-Weeks—No Spanish Needed—Even If You've Never Left The Country."*

Visit the following link to download your Free eBook now:

https://www.timothyzellmer.com/free-ebook.

This ebook has four short steps. They make the moving process clear. They give you insights into navigating migration's hurdles. It does not matter if you don't know Spanish. Get an exclusive discount on migration attorneys in Boquete. Those four steps are a powerful guide through what comes next.

With this knowledge, your move to Boquete is not a leap into the dark. It is a confident stride into the light of a well-informed beginning.

Claim this guide and start your adventure. Begin your transition to a life of ease, culture, and rejuvenation in Boquete, Panama. You are about to see green mountains and smell fresh coffee. We wait for your arrival. It's time to live for less in your slice of paradise. Get going! Get on your way.

## Notice How You've Changed

We began this expedition with the question, "What is the Best Place in the World to Retire?" Boquete, Panama, has emerged as a stellar answer through our exploration. Your retirement is the chapter of life where dreams flourish, and peace is critical. Boquete offers a canvas for painting a better future.

Take the inventory, make your decision, and take action with confidence. Boquete's arms are open; it's time to embrace paradise.

# Appendix

## Important Local Phone Numbers

Emergency Phone Numbers (Teléfonos de Emergencia):

- Police: 104
- Medical Assistance: 911
- Firefighters: 103

Police:

- National Police (Policia Nacional): 728-1914, 728-1356, 6279-5672
- Bajo Boquete: 720-2145, 720-1222

Fire and Ambulance:

- Fire (Cuerpo de Bomberos): 728-3722, 720-1224
- Ambulance: 6728-3098

SINAPROC - Sistema National de Protection Civil (National Civil Protection System) https://www.sinaproc.gob.pa/

Unique Emergency Management System (Sistema Único de Manejo de Emergencias):

- Emergency Number: 911

CSS - Caja Seguro Social Panamá (the Social Insurance Fund for Employees and Dependents) https://www.css.gob.pa/

- Boquete Polyclinic (Policlínica de Boquete): 728-0419

- CSS Ambulance Service (Servicio de Ambulancia CSS): 107

MINSA - Ministerio de Salud de la República de Panamá - Health Center (Centro de Salud) https://www.minsa.gob.pa/

- Phone: 728-0407

Ministerio de Ambiente - Ministry of the Environment https://www.miambiente.gob.pa/

- Phone: 728-0423
- Municipality of Boquete (Município de Boquete)
- Phone: 720-1261
- David Regional Hospital (Hospital Regional de David)
- Phone: 777-8400

Www.RodnyDirect.com - Chiriqui Helpline

- $90/Year Family Subscription
- 24/7/365 Emergency Helpline Service - from anywhere in Panama.
- For Information Only - +507-6573-0141
- Email For More information: info@RodnyDirect.com

AA (Alcoholics Anonymous) in English

Alcoholics Anonymous is a fellowship of men and women coming together to solve their drinking problems. Our primary purpose is to stay sober and help other alcoholics to achieve sobriety.

Boquete ALANO Society - "Providing Support for 12 Step Recovery Programs."

In Person Meetings:

- Monday

- 11 am AA OPEN Discussion
- Tuesday
- 8 am AA CLOSED Discussion
- Wednesday
- 11 am OPEN Big Book- Inclusive. All may participate.
- Friday
- 11 am AA CLOSED Discussion

AA Zoom Discussion:

- Thursday
- 3 pm Discussion

Boquete AA Meetings:

- https://www.aaboquete.org

New Meeting:

- Back to Basics Group
- Thursday 2 pm AA OPEN Discussion

Note on Meetings:

- AA OPEN meetings are available to anyone interested in the Alcoholics Anonymous program of recovery from alcoholism. Nonalcoholics may attend OPEN meetings as observers.
- AA CLOSED meetings are for A.A. members only or for those who have a drinking problem and "have a desire to stop drinking."

AL-ANON Meeting for Families and Friends of Alcoholics:

- Monday

- 1 pm

Please Note:

Al-Anon helps friends and families of alcoholics recover from the impact of living with someone struggling with alcoholism.

# Leave a Review!

Hey there!

I appreciate you taking the time to read my book! Your support truly means a lot to me. If you enjoyed the story and found it helpful, I'd be so grateful if you could spare a moment to drop a review on Amazon. Your feedback not only helps me grow but also guides other readers to discover the book.

How to Leave a Review:

1. Head to the book's page on Amazon. (You will find it by putting *Dr. Timothy Zellmer* in Amazon's search bar)

2. Scroll down to the "Customer Reviews" section.

3. Hit "Write a customer review."

4. Share your thoughts and rate the book. Hey, you can even leave a video review! Just record your thoughts and upload the video along with your written review. It's a fun way to share your experience with fellow readers.

Thanks a bunch for your support!

Warm wishes,

Dr. Timothy Zellmer (Uncle Timmy)

# Acknowledgments

You can skip to the end. It's all blah blah blah, "I love my little sister. She's my favorite." Lol! No! I am kidding. It is worth the read! But I do love my sister, "Big as the Sky!" Keep reading!

The three brothers, we'd taken an oath. We would ignore our parents giving our new baby sister the name *Sarah*. We called her *Cindy* because we were head over heels for *Cindy Hanson*. She was our wonderful babysitter and friend in Canby, Minnesota. That is where I was born, two years and a month before Cindy Sue's dramatic arrival. There are many reasons why her homecoming is my first vivid memory.

They had left, happy and excited for Mom to have the new baby. They said they would return soon. But they weren't coming home! Our mom got Viral Pericarditis right after Cindy was born. She spent weeks in the Chicago hospital's ICU. That is where our dad did his Clinical Pastoral Education after Luther Seminary. He was getting certified to train hospital chaplains. Grandma had to return to the ranch. So, Dad sent for a young lady college student. She arrived by train to take care of us boys. For days, Dad would stop in at bedtime for devotions and to tuck us in. Dad felt scared. Mom was a fighter, clinging to life.

We still hadn't seen her! After days and weeks of promises and delays, Dad explained that Mom and baby Sarah were coming home! But with the possibility of a short visit, having to return to the hospital. Mom was still frail, and my job was to help with the baby. The build-up was killing me! I was little, two years and a month old, jumping around with excitement. My parents had me sit on their bed and wait for them to bring her in to meet me.

I can still see and feel that moment in my mind. Our dad was already an avid photographer and family movie maker (8mm). He was ready with his 35mm camera. It was an Argus Brick mounted to the old paparazzi-style jumbo flash unit. It held a fresh, big blue bulb. We were both ready to pop. While they were in the next room, I raked my nails over their bedspread. It was my thing. So many times, they had asked me to "please stop scratching it.!" It looked like a scene out of the movie *Wolverine*.

The bed comforter had a unique texture, a type you rarely see now. It was fun to touch. It had these tiny, pearl-patterned woven balls along the top. My bedspread-banjo session ended when my parents entered, and my mom placed her on my lap. She was a swaddled-up little thing, only her face and arms showing. She squealed, flapped her new wings twice, sighed, and fell asleep in my arms. Mom smiled at my kid-wrangling skills.

While staring at her, I was thinking about what our dad said, that she might have to return to the hospital. That thought spooked me. I was panicking over the thought that she wouldn't be able to stay. We were to be on our best behavior because Mom was not quite well and still very weak. Dad watched us as an artist, the heavy camera rig in hand, silent, stalking the perfect moment. He only had one bulb to fire off.

In my gentle voice, I asked Mom, "So... How long are we keepin' her?" She shook her head and gave me a confused look. "What, Timmy?" "Is she going back tonight or in a little bit?" "Huh?" Her eyebrows shot up. "Can't Cindy sleep here with us tonight, at least?" "Who?" "Cindy." She gave me a soft, long cooing, "Noooo.. Timmy! No! 'You can keep her *Forever*!'"

I looked up from my kneeling mother at the side of the bed to my father with a full grin. I *Church-Whispered* to him, "Daddy! Momma says I get to keep her forever!" Then I looked up at Dad and turned her a bit so he could see her, my little sleeping *job forever*.

Yep, you could hear the angels singing, *Hallelujah*! He hit the shutter at that perfect moment in time. The flashbulb went off, and we had history. What a great picture! Dad and I could make the crowds swoon on *Movie Nights* with that pic and the story that came with it.

Cindy is my friend, and I am her's. My sister inspires me. She started a *hospice choir!* She retired from teaching and is writing what will be a great book. Many heartwarming stories are about her time as a teacher. She worked with newcomers, refugee camp kids, and such. Some experienced the most terrible things. It is shaping up to be a remarkable story.

Our parents were *Reverend Bruce* and *Ila Zellmer*. It was a mixed marriage: a German Lutheran married a Norwegian Lutheran. Those two gave me the gift of nature. We spent a lot of time at Lake Metigoshe. It's an international lake in the Turtle Mountains. It straddles the Canada-North Dakota border. What my father lacked in Cowboy skills, he more than made up for with boating safety skills. Dad's Chaplain students built Cindy and me our first little rowboat. They did it last summer before we started school.

Shortly after, we got the hang of using our 15-horse Johnson outboard motor. We used it on a full-sized aluminum fishing boat. Dad started my training first, but I gave my little sister private lessons. We hid among the reeds. On that lake, we aced Dad's captain's test. He authorized us to drive boats and tow each other on a surfboard. Passing, he let us drag each other while staying in Danny's Bay. We were proud show-offs, upsetting the neighbors.

"You're too young to be doing that! Do your parents know you kids took their boat out alone?" I would slowly troll by the neighbor's dock with the upset lady, staying a little out of reach. Then, to their astonishment, I would stand proudly and, in my best deep man's voice, say, "Don't worry, ma'am. We both have passed our Captain's test." I liked to see the look on their faces after that!

Danny hailed from Denmark, where you learn to walk so you can hop on a boat. He was my dad's best friend, and they stood up to the neighbors and our mom to defend us and what we were doing. Cindy was a preschooler, and I was a first-grader! When she finally got big enough to pull the starter rope independently, I submitted her for testing. Mom and Gladys (Dan's wife) were 100% against it. Cindy started crying, and they sent us outside to talk in private. They got a little loud.

But when they called us in, it was all arranged. We received rules that offered no second chances and were unbreakable. They trusted our ability to listen, learn, and prioritize safety. I was so thrilled the day she passed. She got it started on the second pull! Dad sat up front. He didn't say a word till she had me towed behind.

He gave us the thumbs-up and hollered, "You did it!" We were both beaming with pride and excitement. From that day on, Cindy and I kept showing off on the water. We got so good at skiing and doing tricks that *Cypress Gardens* tried to recruit us!

Growing up on my grandparents' ranch and farm was something else. My folks embraced my passions. They put up with my long expeditions and deep dives into studies. Their love was evident daily, a feeling that still sticks with me. I'm grateful for their unwavering belief in me.

Dad blessed me to be the last to hear him speak before passing. It was a pretty damn dramatic exit line. "You can do it!" I kept going and now have a hotel and the country of Panama's only drive-thru coffee. Thanks, Dad, for giving me your old-fashioned manual *Royal Typewriter*. You always said I should be a writer. See dad! I am an author. Finally!

Those Royals were so rugged they used to drop them from airplanes! I'm not kidding. Look it up. At home, we all knew when he was writing his sermons. When typing, he shook the house! You passed me a heavy-duty legacy as a writer. I now pass it on to my nephew and friend, *Caleb Weber*.

Thank you, *Uncle John* and *Aunt Connie* (may she rest in peace). Years of fun and friendship have flown by since you moved to Boquete. I never expected to see you two here! What a blast. John, we have done well here for a pair of lost Montana Cowboys. You inspire me with the way you live your life here. I am lucky to have you close by.

I want to shout out to Mike, the incredible *Brains of Boise*, for being there for me from afar during these crazy times. You will only be reading this book because of his technical help. And Mike, you kept me afloat during the pandemic, and you still do. I'm grateful for our friendship. Moments like these make me so glad I made those videos. You are my best *Super Fan/Friend!* I can't wait to see you down here this year!

Another thank you goes out to the friends I made during the pandemic in my *Live Free University* group, a free, live digital sales and marketing group on Facebook. You were my oasis during the pandemic lockdown. I still hope to see you all here in Panama. And no, I am not going anywhere—no matter what!

I'm grateful to the *Boquete Authors Group* and all its members, past, present, and deceased. I've found my voice as a writer. I experienced this while diving into the world of top poets, authors, and editors. Theirs is a beautiful world. The dedication and talent of this group humble me. Thank you, everyone.

I have seen awe-inspiring creators emerge from this collective. You know, four exceptional folks in our club deserve a special shoutout. First up is *Levi Clarence Pinzon*, my adopted nephew (Indigenous style). He is an author of Ngäbe Children's Books. Thanks, Levi, for your unfailing friendship and support of my writing. And thank you for taking my grandpa Levi's middle name (Clarence) as your own. That makes us, I guess, family doubled.

I want to give a massive shoutout to *Dwayne* for his incredible author training. Thank you for your support and inspiration. You have been a tremendous driving force behind me. Your steady hand helped me push through to publishing. I can't thank you enough, Dwayne!

One of the most diligent working members is an Amazon Best Seller, my friend, *Brinn Colenda*. Check him out. He is the award-winning author of the "Callahan Family Saga." This series highlights families under stress, particularly military families. He has a military and aviation history as a jet fighter jock/instructor. He also has exceptional writing skills from training at Oxford University. You inspire me with the quality of your writing.

I love his latest offering, *"The Irish Skateboard Club."* It crosses over to Young Adult/Adult romance thriller territory. That guy can tell a tale you get lost in.

My buddy is the famous *Dr. Fred Minton*. He's a cowboy doctor, too! He's a Ph.D. Psychologist and my pal. He is badass and 89! He is a multi-book published Amazon author and a real Boquete

186

Renaissance Man; he blogs and vlogs! He is my most successful coaching student. He rocked the field for the Dodgers Baseball Team. He played beside his mirror-identical twin!

He wrote a book about me and my cowboy grandpa, Levi Clarence Johnson, during one of his many stays in my Hotel! That is why you are seeing "Dr." before my name. He saw the cover of this book and dug in his heels over my honorifics/titles. He said, "*The Real You* needs to get branded on the spine of this book. Stand up for who you are and what you've done. Don't shy away from your accomplishments. You *are Dr. Tim!*"

Here is a fun fact: Dr. Fred Minton's and my work as a Psychologist and Dentist somehow got mixed up back in Oklahoma City. Those children he was treating were *Wards of the State*. I had them stacked twenty towers full, from kid's prison to truancy campers.

Dr. Fred and I never met face-to-face in Oklahoma. We only spoke once by phone back then, and our staff did all the talking. For years, we practiced three city blocks away from each other. He had "The Reading Center," code for *Children's Psychological Services*. Those kids would always tell me how much they loved him and how he was helping them with school and their feelings.

He has done the same for me. Lucky me! We always made the other's appointments late! Lol! We ghosted in and out of each other's lives only to finally meet in Boquete and discover the rest of the story. We both sang the baritone line at Pastor Stan's old church in Boquete. We liked sitting together in the Singing-Cowboy-Doctor section. One Sunday, chatting before church, we discovered the connection linking our lives. It is a small world.

**Pro Tip:** Pick a niche lesson. The final word is *on Fred*. He produces *high-interest, low-vocabulary* (with graphics) books for young people. My sister says we need a lot more of these. And she knows everything—well, everything that is important. It is a pretty easy niche to serve. There is not much competition. And there is high demand. It looks like an opportunity. The U.S. is being flooded right now with young immigrants who need to learn English.

Thank you, Samuli. You have helped me fight my demons and overcome resistance. I am grateful for your ability to listen to my stories, understand my questions, and give great advice. "Resistance is Futile!"- says Samuli and *Locutus* of the Borg (from Star Trek).

Finally, I must thank my many YouTube *Super Fans* worldwide. What a delightful tribe we formed! The incredible richness you have brought to my life is staggering. The tiny bits of joy my videos gave you do not compare to what you gave me. I was able to make friends from everywhere. "You are like you are in your videos!" How could I not be? "You are the same chill guy, walking and talking, in paradise!" I love your stories. I love it when you reach out.

And thanks to *Dr. Sam Savage,* my *Grammy*-winning voice coach and friend! (Did anyone else read the adventure book series or see the show *Doc Savage - The Man in Bronze?*). I am starting to sound like Robert Goulet on a good day. So, prepare yourself for some great *Reto-Trovedores*, the Competitive Panamanian Yodeling Videos! (Good God! You can't make this stuff up!) I would never have met you, Sam, if I hadn't done those videos. Your words and voice are the inspiring stuff that fills my singing dreams.

Also, I am talking to you guys out on that Israeli desert Kibbutz, raising all the chickens and kids! I'm so happy you saw all our green jungles and flowers. I can't imagine living in a bare desert like you, your three kids, and your husband do. You made me understand why my YouTube videos were so important. You had to come to meet me, stay a while in my hotel, and immerse yourselves in Boquete!

The mom said, "Your videos are like coming up for air; it is amazing that everything here is so green! You made a window into another world." One son confided, "She's obsessed! We've seen all your videos! She plays them over and over again. You are why we're here."

And I wish to say a kind word about my good friend David, a fine fellow, a Norwegian-Lutheran born in Minnesota like me. I'm so sorry you got called home early to baby Jesus. I am happy I got to know you and you could come down here a few times. You were kind to me. Thank you, my friend.

Thank you one and all. Your words and deeds have enriched my life and filled my creative gas tank. So many of you carried me through the troubles of the last few years with your kind messages and calls. It's funny, but I've never been in the same room with some of my best friends.

Thank you very much, Panama! It has been a wonderful experience moving here to the crossroads called Boquete. It is all rubbing off on me. It may be me or the people here. I am in sync with the place. For me, I see fun in all directions. I love the friendliness of the Panamanians. That is why I have met so many people here—the camaraderie, the sense of community, and the feeling of belonging. You gave me that. A chance to come in the backdoor, sit, eat, drink coffee, chat, and get to know each other.

And to the Panama Indigenous, thank you very, very much. I have lived now beyond my wildest childhood dreams. Where my eyes have seen and what my heart has felt, no lost *Viking Boy* raised by *Indians* ever did. To have lived inside your world. I am forever grateful to the many Indigenous nations of all the Americas."

Thank you also to my adopted godson, *Cristobal*. Oh, how your heart shines bright in joyful service to Panama. Our wild adventures won't fit in this book. The Commanders of the *Buko-Day,* the *Ngäbe-Buglé Comarcal Security Forces,* gave us new names. He was *Commander Chitiküm* (sounds like She-tee-goon), and mine was *Dr. Chuma*! When he says, "We got *Baptized into the Tribe*!" That makes me laugh!

Cristobal asked excitedly, "So, what do our names mean?" The head commander looked confused. "Does it mean something fearsome like *Jumping Jaguar* or *Biting Snake*?" Lol! He explained that these were not names like Kevin Costner got—*Dances with Wolves*.

No! These were the names of good, well-known Ngäbe people no longer living. They weren't using their names anymore. It was a simple Ngäbe memory aid. They are names as familiar as *Bob* or *Joe*. It's funny when the kids lay hiding in the jungle waiting for our arrival, all whispering as one, "Chuma, Chuma, Chuma!" Some of my Ngöbe friends in Boquete do the same.

That reminds me of Joe, the old Indigenous cowboy keeping my horse pastured at his ranch. I had a rule: I would only work in their IHS hospital or clinic once they got me a safe place for my horse. It had to be for the first two weeks. "I am sorry, Dr. Zellmer. We do health care, not horse boarding!" It was my trick to get in the backdoor. I'd say, "Are you telling me your tribe is the only one without a nice old famous rancher, rodeo, bronc buster kind of guy?"

If a stunned silence continued, I threw them a dandy that always got results. "You call me back by tomorrow with someone's phone number. Then, I will call and check out your Cowboy-Indian first before telling you I'm coming. And you better call the Surgeon General's office. Ask them about me. They know me. They won't want you to lose me. They have a list of over 70 Indian Health Service Dentist spots who need me. Sorry for the odd request. I can sleep in my truck, but my horse sure can't."

I would arrive on the weekend to show my face. I would chase cows around their Rez with the Old Rancher and his family. On Monday, it was my first day at their tribe's Dental Clinic. The comments were all the same: "You're not a Dentist! You're a damn cowboy! I saw you out on Joe's ranch last weekend. Are you a real Dentist? You sure look different in that white doctor's coat!"

The first night, I sat silent for a long time, watching the sunset with old Joe. He was not a talker. I had a question: "So, what are the people here like?" With elder wisdom, he answered my question. What were they like on the reservation you came from?" I smiled and said, "They were great! They are wonderful people!

He thought long and said, "You will find them here the same." Then, for the first time since I arrived in the morning, he looked me in the eye and smiled. "Don't worry, birds of a feather flock together." That seemed to end our little talk, so we both stared off at the final edge of the sun as it slid behind the horizon. In classic Indigenous code-switching (Tribal Grammar), a full minute paused, he closed with, "Yes. It is so!"

Made in the USA
Coppell, TX
19 October 2024

38891129R00108